YOUR RIGHTS AS A TENANT

by
Margaret C. Jasper

Oceana's Legal Almanac Series:
Law for the Layperson

Oceana Publications

You may order this or any other Oxford University Press publication by visiting the Oxford University Press and Oceana websites at www.oup.com and www.oceanalaw.com respectively.

Library of Congress Control Number: 2006935510

ISBN 978-0-19-532362-7

Oceana's Legal Almanac Series: Law for the Layperson
ISSN 1075-7376

©2007 Oxford University Press, Inc.

Manufactured in the United States of America on acid-free paper.

To My Husband Chris

Your love and support
are my motivation and inspiration

-and-

In memory of my son, Jimmy

Table of Contents

CHAPTER 5:
SECURITY DEPOSITS

CHAPTER 6:
HEALTH, SAFETY AND HABITABILITY

CHAPTER 7:
RENTER'S INSURANCE

APPENDICES

ABOUT THE AUTHOR

MARGARET C. JASPER is an attorney engaged in the general practice of law in South Salem, New York, concentrating in the areas of personal injury and entertainment law. Ms. Jasper holds a Juris Doctor degree from Pace University School of Law, White Plains, New York, is a member of the New York and Connecticut bars, and is certified to practice before the United States District Courts for the Southern and Eastern Districts of New York, the United States Court of Appeals for the Second Circuit, and the United States Supreme Court.

Ms. Jasper has been appointed to the law guardian panel for the Family Court of the State of New York, is a member of a number of professional organizations and associations, and is a New York State licensed real estate broker operating as Jasper Real Estate, in South Salem, New York.

Margaret Jasper maintains a website at http://www.JasperLawOffice.com.

In 2004, Ms. Jasper successfully argued a case before the New York Court of Appeals which gives mothers of babies who are stillborn due to medical negligence the right to bring a legal action and recover emotional distress damages. This successful appeal overturned a 26-year-old New York case precedent, that previously prevented mothers of stillborn babies to sue their negligent medical providers.

Ms. Jasper is the author and general editor of the following legal almanacs:

AIDS Law

The Americans with Disabilities Act

Animal Rights Law

Auto Leasing

Bankruptcy Law for the Individual Debtor

Banks and their Customers

Becoming a Citizen

Buying and Selling Your Home

Commercial Law

Consumer Rights Law

Co-ops and Condominiums: Your Rights and Obligations as Owner

Copyright Law

Credit Cards and the Law

Custodial Rights

Dealing with Debt

Dictionary of Selected Legal Terms

Drunk Driving Law

DWI, DUI and the Law

Education Law

Elder Law

Employee Rights in the Workplace

Employment Discrimination Under Title VII

Environmental Law

Estate Planning

Everyday Legal Forms

Executors and Personal Representatives: Rights and Responsibilities

Harassment in the Workplace

Health Care and Your Rights

Health Care Directives

Hiring Household Help and Contractors: Your Rights and Obligations Under the Law

Home Mortgage Law Primer

Hospital Liability Law

How To Change Your Name

How To Protect Your Challenged Child

How To Start Your Own Business

Identity Theft and How To Protect Yourself

Individual Bankruptcy and Restructuring

Injured on the Job: Employee Rights, Worker's Compensation and Disability Insurance Law

International Adoption

Juvenile Justice and Children's Law

Labor Law

Landlord-Tenant Law

Law for the Small Business Owner

The Law of Attachment and Garnishment

The Law of Buying and Selling

The Law of Capital Punishment

The Law of Child Custody

The Law of Contracts

The Law of Debt Collection

The Law of Dispute Resolution

The Law of Immigration

The Law of Libel and Slander

The Law of Medical Malpractice

The Law of No-Fault Insurance

The Law of Obscenity and Pornography

The Law of Personal Injury

The Law of Premises Liability

The Law of Product Liability

The Law of Speech and the First Amendment

The Law of Violence Against Women

Lemon Laws

Living Together: Practical Legal Issues

Marriage and Divorce

Missing and Exploited Children: How to Protect Your Child

Motor Vehicle Law

Nursing Home Negligence

Patent Law

Pet Law

Prescription Drugs

Privacy and the Internet: Your Rights and Expectations Under the Law

Probate Law

Real Estate Law for the Homeowner and Broker

Religion and the Law

Retirement Planning

The Right to Die

Rights of Single Parents

Small Claims Court

Social Security Law

Special Education Law

Teenagers and Substance Abuse

Trademark Law

Trouble Next Door: What to do With Your Neighbor

Victim's Rights Law

Welfare: Your Rights and the Law

What if It Happened to You: Violent Crimes and Victims' Rights

What if the Product Doesn't Work: Warranties & Guarantees

Workers' Compensation Law

Your Child's Legal Rights: An Overview

Your Rights in a Class Action Suit

Your Rights as a Tenant

Your Rights Under the Family and Medical Leave Act

You've Been Fired: Your Rights and Remedies

INTRODUCTION

This almanac presents an overview of the law governing tenant's rights, beginning with the search for rental property, the application process, credit and background checks, fair housing and discrimination issues, negotiating the lease terms, and security deposits. This almanac also discusses the landlord-tenant relationship, and sets forth the basic legal rights afforded the tenant under the law. The tenant's rights and responsibilities during the lease period are also explored. This almanac also sets forth the circumstances under which the landlord-tenant relationship may end, including abandonment, voluntary termination, and eviction proceedings. In addition, the tenant's rights during a co-op/condominium conversion of the rental property are also discussed.

The Appendix provides applicable statutes, sample forms, and other pertinent information and data. The Glossary contains definitions of many of the terms used throughout the almanac.

CHAPTER 1:
OVERVIEW OF THE LANDLORD-TENANT RELATIONSHIP

WHAT IS A LANDLORD?

A landlord is the owner of rental property that is leased to another person, known as a "tenant." The rental property is generally a house, an apartment, a condominium, co-op, or room. The landlord's interest in the rental property is known as a *freehold* estate. A landlord may be either a fee simple owner of land—i.e., absolute ownership without limitation or condition—or simply a person who has an assignable interest in the property

The landlord leases the property to the tenant in exchange for the payment of money, known as *rent*. The tenant obtains the right to the exclusive use and possession of the rental property during the lease period for the purpose of making it his or her home. The landlord is also referred to as the *lessor* of the rental property.

In some instances, the landlord or owner hires a property manager to act as an agent on his behalf in managing the rental property. In that case, the tenant deals directly with the property agent instead of the landlord.

WHAT IS A TENANT?

As discussed above, the tenant is the individual who has been given the right to use and occupy the rental property pursuant to the terms and conditions of the rental agreement, also referred to as a *lease* The tenant is referred to as the *lessee* of the rental property. The tenant's interest in the leased property is known as a *non-freehold* or *leasehold* estate.

As long as the tenant abides by the terms and conditions of the lease, he or she is entitled to the exclusive possession of the rental property for the term of the lease. The specific period of time varies according to the type of lease entered into between the parties. The time period may be indefinite—e.g., a month-to-month tenancy—or for a specified term, e.g., 3 years.

GOVERNING LAW

The law that governs the relationship between the landlord and the tenant and the rental of residential property is simply known as *landlord-tenant law*. Landlord-tenant law is derived from both statutory law and the common law—i.e., judge-made law.

A table of state tenants' rights statutes is set forth at Appendix 1 of this almanac.

Many states have patterned their landlord-tenant law after the Uniform Residential Landlord And Tenant Act (URLTA), which is more fully discussed in Chapter 10 of this almanac.

TYPES OF TENANCIES

The four basic types of non-freehold estate are as follows:

Tenancy for Years

Tenancy for years—also known as an estate for years—is the most common type of leasehold interest in real property. A tenancy for years is created for a definite, time period, where both the beginning and end of the tenancy term is fixed. The tenancy automatically terminates when the time period ends. Nevertheless, a tenancy for years may end earlier if there is a breach of the lease agreement, e.g., the tenant fails to pay rent.

Periodic Tenancy

Periodic tenancy is one which continues from one period to the next, e.g., month-to-month or week-to-week. The period of the tenancy is generally inferred by how often rent is paid, however, such a tenancy can also be created by express agreement between the parties.

Unlike the tenancy for years, a periodic tenancy has no termination date, but continues indefinitely until one of the parties decides to terminate the agreement, upon advance notice to the other party. Such notice is generally required to be given for the same duration as the period of the tenancy. For example, in a month-to-month tenancy, one month notice of termination is generally required, and for a week-to-week tenancy, one week notice is generally required. However, many states now require a 3-day notice for all such tenancies, regardless of the period involved.

A periodic tenancy may be created following the automatic termination of a tenancy for years. For example, at the end of the fixed lease period, if the tenant does not move out, he or she is known as a "holdover" tenant. The landlord has the option of evicting the tenant or letting the tenant stay. If the landlord opts to let the tenant remain without a lease, a periodic tenancy is created.

Tenancy at Will

Tenancy at will is one which has no fixed duration, and which, under the common law, may be terminated at any time, by either party, without notice. Generally, the tenant is permitted reasonable time to remove his or her property from the premises. Nevertheless, the difference between a tenancy at will and a periodic tenancy has been largely eradicated because many states now statutorily require landlords to give at-will tenants the same right to advance notice as a periodic tenant is given.

Tenancy at Sufferance

Tenancy at sufferance arises when a tenant "holds over"—i.e., fails to vacate the rental property—when the lease expires. The landlord then has the right to either evict the tenant or hold the tenant to another term of the same duration as the expired lease.

If the landlord does not wish to hold the tenant to another lease term, the landlord can treat the holdover tenant as a trespasser. If the tenant continues to pay rent, and the landlord accepts the rental payment, a periodic tenancy may be created as discussed above.

Some courts, however, have strictly interpreted such an arrangement as an election by the landlord to hold the tenant over for an entirely new lease term. If the landlord does make such an election, all of the terms and conditions of the previous lease are binding, including the amount of rent.

TENANTS' ASSOCIATIONS

A tenants' association is formed when a group of tenants in a building or complex decide to organize for the purpose of discussing and resolving landlord-tenant problems. Although there are a variety of ways in which a tenants' association can operate, it is common for the tenants to elect a committee. The committee meets regularly to address issues concerning the tenants, and intercede with the landlord on behalf of the tenants.

More organized tenants' associations may also hold forums for tenants to inform them of their rights and responsibilities, and distribute a newsletter to advise the tenants of the committee's activities. Common issues a tenants' association attempts to resolve with a landlord include rent increases, repairs and maintenance, and security issues.

CHAPTER 2:
THE SEARCH FOR RENTAL PROPERTY

YOUR RENTAL PROPERTY CRITERIA

Before you start your search for rental property, you should make a list of the criteria you desire for the place you will call home. Consider where you want to live, e.g., close to your job, close to family, close to shopping, etc. If you have children, the quality of the school district may be an important factor. How much can you afford in rent? How large of an apartment do you need? Do you have a pet?

It is also important to consider the type and length of lease suitable for the tenant's short and long-term plans, e.g., a tenancy for years or a periodic tenancy, etc.

As you go through your list, you will be able to avoid wasting time looking at apartments that are not suitable for you.

Affordability

Before shopping for an apartment, figure out how much of your income you can comfortably allocate towards rent, including utilities and other related expenses. Firmly commit yourself to this figure and visit rental units that are within your established range. Some considerations include:

1. The rental amount;

2. Whether utilities are included in the rent; and

3. The amount and availability of funds for a security deposit, which is generally the equivalent of one to two months' rent.

It is unwise to look at rentals that are out of your price range, as you don't want to be tempted by a property that will only cause financial trouble for you down the road.

Characteristics

There are many kinds of properties available for rent, such as apartments in small buildings or skyscrapers, lofts, 1 and 2-family homes, garden apartments, cottages, etc. You must consider the type of property that most suits your needs. If you work out of your home, you may need extra space for an office. If you have children and/or pets, you may want to look for a private home with a large backyard. If you are a gourmet cook, the kitchen may be your priority. If you are disabled, accessibility may be the overriding concern. Before you begin your search, make sure you list all of your priorities, starting with the essentials.

Location

Location is often one of the most important factors in finding a place to live. If you have a specific area in mind, take time to walk through the neighborhood so you can get a feel for the community to see if it appeals to you. You should observe whether the properties are well-maintained, and how the people interact. Are they friendly or do they keep to themselves? Which do you prefer? Is the population primarily made up of senior citizens or families with children? Do you feel at home? If possible, speak with your prospective neighbors in the building you are considering and find out whether they have any complaints about the landlord, building management, repair and maintenance services, etc.

If you are not sure where you would like to live, in order to narrow down your choices, make a list of the neighborhood features that are most important to you. For example, if you don't drive and need to depend on mass transportation, this will help focus your search. If you own one or more vehicles, parking may be an issue, therefore you should avoid rental properties that do not provide a garage space, designated parking space, or ample street parking. If you like quiet surroundings, don't move into an urban area. If you have children, you may be concerned about what the school district has to offer. Don't fall in love with an apartment in a neighborhood that has few or none of the amenities you have on your list. Chances are you will not be happy with your choice in the long run.

School District

There are a number of ways to research the quality of your prospective school district. Most rental agents can supply you with information about the local schools. In addition, you can usually find out important statistical data—e.g., test scores, academic standing, dropout rates, etc.—from the state department of education.

You should also visit the school which your child will be attending to observe the surroundings and obtain more specific information, such as class size, teacher qualifications, availability of extracurricular activities, etc.

BEGIN THE SEARCH

Visit the Neighborhood

A good way of finding rental property is to visit the neighborhood you would like to reside in and look for rental signs. Many apartment complexes have management offices or superintendents who may be aware of available or soon-to be vacant units in the building. Check for available rentals on bulletin boards in local supermarkets, town offices, libraries, etc. You can also post your own "apartment wanted" signs.

Apartment Locator Services

If you don't have the time to search for appropriate rental housing, there are services that will look for available properties matching your criteria. Also known as a prepaid rental listing service, the business will generally sell you a list of available rental units purportedly based upon the criteria you provide.

It is important that the rental information be current and accurate, and that the service guarantee that they will provide a minimum number of listings. These businesses are generally subject to government regulation and licensing requirements, thus, the reader is advised to check the law of his or her own jurisdiction concerning the protections afforded prospective tenants when dealing with prepaid rental listing services.

Before signing an agreement, such as a finder's fee contract, make sure you know how much the service will cost you. Some services charge a relatively moderate flat fee in return for a list of available rental units in a certain location, and some charge much higher fees.

It is important to check out the background of the service before you sign a contract and hand over any money. Check with the Better Business Bureau to see whether there have been any complaints about the service. Some apartment-finders offer outdated information or provide leads that you could have obtained on your own by consulting the real estate section of your location newspaper at no cost.

Real Estate Brokers

Many real estate brokers maintain rental listings on behalf of property owners. You should carefully select your real estate broker. Make sure he or she has a lot of experience and a good reputation. Check with the

Better Business Bureau to find out whether there have been any complaints made against the real estate broker. Find out how much of a fee you will be charged and how it is computed, e.g. a flat fee or a certain percentage of the first year's rent. Make sure you provide the real estate broker with your list of priorities so they can narrow down their search. Don't waste time on properties that don't meet your requirements.

Classified Advertisements

Regularly check the classified advertisements of your local newspapers. Many newspapers have a particular day when they concentrate on real estate, including rentals. Many newspapers also list their classified advertisements on the Internet. The online advertisements may be the most up-to-date listings available.

In addition, some areas carry publications that contain rental listings, which are often published and distributed by local real estate offices.

Personal Recommendations

Another way to find rental property is through word of mouth. Get leads from your friends, relatives, and co-workers. Let people know you are searching for an apartment. People are often aware of apartment availability in their building or a house for rent in your target neighborhood.

VIEWING THE RENTAL PROPERTY

A rental property may be available for viewing either by open house, when many prospective renters are invited to view the property at the same time, or by appointment with the landlord or, if listed, with the real estate broker who has the rental listing. When viewing properties, bring your list of priorities with you so you can determine whether the property meets your criteria.

You should also bring all of the information you will need to fill out the rental application, such as employment history, credit information and contact information for your references. If available, bring a copy of your credit report and written reference letters, such as character references.

A sample character reference letter is set forth at Appendix 2 of this almanac.

You should also inquire about your prospective neighbors. Ask the landlord whether anyone in the building has any type of criminal background. You can perform your own background check online. In addition, every state has a sex offender registration website where you can determine whether any of the listed offenders reside in your neighborhood.

Inspecting the Property

Once you have decided on a particular rental property, it is important to carefully inspect the condition of the property with the landlord or the property management agent present. Potential problems include:

1. Holes or cracks in the walls, ceiling, floor, etc.;

2. Moist areas that may indicate water damage or leaks;

3. Water problems, such as rusty or discolored water, or hot water deficiency;

4. Heating and air conditioning problems;

5. Electrical problems, e.g., defective wiring or an insufficient number of outlets, etc.;

6. Damaged furniture if the rental is furnished;

7. Evidence of infestation;

8. Trash removal problems;

9. Environmental problems, e.g., evidence of asbestos which poses serious health hazards if inhaled, or lead paint which can cause lead poisoning and serious health defects in children who ingest chipped paint particles; and

10. The overall cleanliness of the property and its common areas, such as the halls and incinerator rooms.

It is advisable to make a written inventory of the property—e.g., noting existing damage, and repairs which the landlord agrees to make—which should be dated and signed by all parties. You should also take photographs or videotape the property prior to moving in. This may prove helpful in case there is a dispute about the rental's move-in condition when you seek reimbursement of the security deposit.

When renting a house, it is important to find out who is responsible for maintaining the exterior of the property, e.g., lawn maintenance, snow removal, and general repairs. If the tenant is responsible, this will necessarily increase the overall cost of renting the property.

THE RENTAL APPLICATION

Most landlords require prospective tenants to complete a rental application. A rental application is a form that requests information concerning an individual's occupation, income, credit worthiness, and references. It is used by the landlord to determine whether or not he or she wishes to rent his or her property to the applicant.

Be prepared to answer all of the questions listed on the rental application, such as contact information for your personal and credit references, employment history, prior landlords, income, bank account information, etc. Your prospective landlord will use the information provided to decide whether to rent the property to you. Your income to debt ratio and credit history is a very important factor. Landlords want to make sure their tenants are not credits risks. If you are self-employed, the landlord will likely ask for proof of your income, such as tax returns.

Information generally found on a rental application include:

1. Employment history, including the names, addresses, and telephone numbers of present and past employers.

2. Rental history, including the names, addresses, and telephone numbers of your current and past landlords.

3. The names, addresses, and telephone numbers of your personal references.

4. Identifying information, such as your driver's license number and social security number.

5. Financial information, including income sources, bank name and address, and bank account numbers.

6. Credit information, including the names and addresses of all creditors and account numbers, and an authorization to obtain a credit report from a credit reporting agency.

It is illegal for a rental application to request information concerning one's race, color, national origin, ancestry, religion, sex, sexual preference, age, disability status, marital status, or whether there are children under the age of 18 in the household. The subject of unlawful housing discrimination is discussed more fully in Chapter 3 of this almanac.

Nevertheless, it is generally permissible to ask the prospective tenant how many people will be living in the property to prevent overcrowding. State statutes may set occupancy limits, however, as a practical matter, the landlord can require a reasonable standard for the number of people per square feet in the property, although this standard cannot be used as a pretext for refusing to rent to households with children, if the landlord would rent to a household with the identical number of adult occupants.

Also, you can expect the landlord to do a background investigation based on the information you provide. Make sure the references you list on your rental application know that you have provided their contact information so they are not caught off guard. The persons your prospective landlord may contact will probably want to make sure you gave your permission for the landlord to call and request information. Therefore, the rental application will likely include your written permission for the landlord to speak with your references.

Do not misrepresent your situation when you complete the rental application. Don't exaggerate your income or downplay your debts. It's very easy for your landlord to verify the information you provide. If your prospective landlord finds out you shaded the truth on your rental application, your application will likely be rejected.

A landlord may charge a prospective tenant a fee for processing a rental application. The fee is used to offset the costs of investigating the information on the application and obtaining the credit report. However, a fee in excess of the landlord's actual costs is generally not permissible. In addition, the prospective tenant is entitled to know how long the rental application review process will take.

A sample rental application is set forth at Appendix 3 of this almanac.

YOUR CREDIT REPORT

Your prospective landlord will likely want to order their own copy of your credit report directly from the credit reporting agency, and charge you a fee for ordering the report, although he or she may be willing to accept a copy of your most recent credit report.

Your credit report may serve as one of the most important indicators of your financial responsibility, which assists the landlord in making a decision to rent. The credit report demonstrates whether you pay your bills on time, whether there are any judgments against you, whether you have filed bankruptcy, and other financial and credit information. The credit report only divulges information available during a legally permissible review period—e.g., 7 to 10 years, depending on the type of information.

A landlord can legitimately reject a tenant based on a negative credit report, therefore, it is a good idea to obtain a copy of one's own credit report prior to completing the rental application to make sure that it is accurate, to take the opportunity to correct any inaccuracies, and to provide explanations for any negative information appearing in the report.

The Disposal Rule

Pursuant to the "Disposal Rule," all businesses, including individual landlords, are required to take steps to safeguard and eventually destroy credit reports and any information they have that is derived from an individual's credit report. The Federal Trade Commission (FTC) issued the Disposal Rule, which went into effect on June 1, 2005, when it implemented the *Fair and Accurate Credit Transaction Act* (the "FACT Act").

Under the Disposal Rule, a credit report must be kept in a secure location to minimize the chance the information will be used by another for illegal purposes, such as identity theft. When the landlord no longer has a legitimate business reason to keep the tenant's credit report, it must be routinely destroyed. The manner of destruction must be reasonable, i.e., a shredder. In addition, any computer files must be deleted.

If a landlord or other business wilfully disregards the Disposal Rule, the landlord could be liable to the tenant for any actual damages suffered, including attorney fees, costs of litigation, and punitive damages, as well as fines assessed by the FTC.

REJECTION

A landlord may reject a prospective tenant for a number of reasons, or for no reason at all, provided the landlord does not unlawfully discriminate against the prospective tenant. For example, a landlord may reject a tenant if the tenant's income is so low it makes it unlikely that he or she will be able to pay the rent. A landlord may also reject a tenant for whom the landlord has received negative references, e.g., a prior landlord reports that the prospective tenant habitually paid their rent late or continually violated lease provisions. In addition, a tenant may be rejected if they engage in illegal behavior or have prior criminal convictions. In fact, a tenant may be rejected if they smoke provided the landlord has a no-smoking policy for all tenants who live in the building.

A landlord is not obligated to tell a prospective tenant the reasons he or she did not qualify for the rental. However, if the decision was based, in whole or in part, on negative information contained in the credit report, the landlord is legally required to supply the prospective tenant with the name and contact information for the credit agency that reported the negative information. In addition, the landlord must advise the individual that he or she is entitled to a copy of that report from the credit reporting agency at no cost. Upon request, the landlord is also obligated to give the prospective tenant a copy of his or her report.

Contact information for the three major national credit bureaus is as follows:

EQUIFAX
P.O. Box 740241
Atlanta, GA 30374
Tel: (800) 685-1111
Website: www.equifax.com

EXPERIAN
701 Experian Parkway
Allen, TX 75013
Tel: (888) 397-3742
Website: www.experian.com

TRANS UNION
P.O. Box 1000
Chester, PA 19022
Tel: (800) 916-8800
Website: www.transunion.com

THE RENTAL DEPOSIT

If the landlord agrees to rent the property to the tenant, but the tenant is unable to take immediate possession of the property, the landlord may request the tenant to place a deposit on the rental—known as a "holding deposit"—for a certain period of time until the tenant pays the necessary security deposit and initial rental payment. The holding deposit is generally nonrefundable if the tenant backs out of the deal.

The holding deposit is used to offset the expenses incurred by the landlord in taking the rental property off the market, such as lost rental income. The landlord is then free to rent the property to another. If the holding deposit is given to the landlord at the time the rental application is submitted, but before the applicant is accepted, the landlord is required to return the entire deposit to the applicant if the landlord subsequently decides not to rent to the applicant.

PUBLIC HOUSING

Public housing was established to provide decent and safe rental housing for eligible low-income families, the elderly, and persons with disabilities. Public housing comes in all sizes and types, from scattered single-family homes to high-rise apartment buildings. In addition, housing choice vouchers allow very low-income families to choose and lease or purchase safe, decent, and affordable privately-owned rental housing. There are approximately 1.3 million households living in public housing units.

Eligibility

Public housing is limited to low-income families and individuals. Eligibility criteria include annual gross income; status as elderly or disabled; and citizenship or immigration status. The public housing agency will also check an applicant's references.

The income limits for public housing are set by the Department of Housing and Urban Development (HUD). HUD sets the lower income limits at 80%—and very low income limits at 50%—of the median income depending on the unit in which the applicant wants to live. Income limits vary from area to area, and may depend on family size.

Application Process

If you would like to apply for public housing, you should contact your local HUD office. Your application must be written, and includes the following information:

1. Personal information for all persons who will be living in the rental property, including their names, gender, date of birth, and relationship to the household;

2. Your present address and telephone number;

3. Family characteristics that might qualify a family for tenant selection preferences, such as a veteran's preference;

4. Names and addresses of your current and previous landlords for information about your family's suitability as a tenant;

5. Projected income over the next 12 months and the source of that income;

6. Contact information for employers, financial institutions, etc.; and

7. An estimate of your family's anticipated income for the next twelve months and the sources of that income.

The public housing agent will generally require you to supply documentation, such as tax returns, for the purpose of verifying the information you entered on your rental application. Public housing authorities may also ask to visit your home to interview you and observe how you maintain your current residence.

The public housing authority is required to provide you, in writing, whether you have been accepted or rejected as a tenant. If you are deemed eligible for public housing, your name will be put on a waiting list and you will be contacted once your name is reached. If you are deemed ineligible, you are entitled to know why, and you can request an informal hearing.

If you are accepted as tenant in a public housing building, you will have to sign a lease with the housing authority, along with any required security deposit. The lease should be carefully reviewed and any questions answered to your satisfaction before you sign the lease.

Rent for public housing is based on a family's projected gross annual income, including income earned by the head of household, his or her spouse, and any family members over the age of 18. The annual income is reduced by any deductions or exclusions. For example, HUD excludes a certain dollar amount for each dependent; for elderly or disabled individuals, and some medical deductions for families headed by an elderly or disabled person.

CHAPTER 3:
FAIR HOUSING AND DISCRIMINATION

IN GENERAL

Federal, state and local fair housing laws provide protection to prospective tenants against housing discrimination. These laws set forth the illegal reasons to refuse to rent to a tenant. Landlords are still free to choose among prospective tenants, as long as their decisions comply with these laws and are based on legitimate business criteria.

For example, a landlord is entitled to reject an individual who has a bad credit history, insufficient income to pay the rent, or past negative behavior—such as having caused property damage—that makes the person a bad risk. A valid occupancy policy limiting the number of people per rental, based on health and safety concerns, or on the rental property's plumbing or electrical capacities, may also be a legal basis for refusing tenants.

ILLEGAL DISCRIMINATION

It is illegal for a landlord to refuse to rent to a tenant on the basis of group characteristics specified by law that are not closely related to the business needs of the landlord. In general, discrimination based on the following factors have been deemed illegal under various federal and state statutes:

1. Race

2. Color

3. Religion

4. Gender

5. Marital status

6. National origin

7. Ancestry

8. Familial status

9. Mental disability

10. Physical disability

11. Sexual orientation

Further, although it is illegal for landlords to discriminate against families with children, specially designated senior citizen housing may set a minimum age requirement for all occupants.

Even though landlords are entitled to ask business-related questions on a rental application or during an interview, they must subject all applicants to the identical set of basic questions. Interview or application questions that aren't directed at everyone constitute special treatment.

For example, landlords who ask a prospective tenant how they arrived in this country must ask all tenants the same question, not just those whom they suspect might be an illegal immigrant. Similarly, a landlord cannot require a credit report from only one class of prospective tenants, e.g., men of Hispanic origin, as that would be considered discriminatory.

The reader is advised to check the law of his or her own jurisdiction concerning the categories of discrimination that are deemed illegal, as some states may afford greater coverage than others.

Exception

Owner-occupied, single-family homeowners who rent out a single room in the home to a lodger, where there are no other lodgers living in the household, are not subject to some of the restrictions on illegal discrimination. Nevertheless, the owner cannot make oral or written statements, or use notices or advertisements that indicate any preference, limitation, or discriminatory practice. However, a person in a single-family home seeking a roommate may express a gender preference if there will be common living areas.

REMEDIES

As further discussed below, a victim of discrimination may file a housing discrimination complaint with the United States Department of Housing and Urban Development (HUD). HUD will investigate the complaint and take action if warranted. If the discrimination is a violation of a state fair housing law, the tenant may wish to file a complaint with the state agency in charge of enforcing the law. Instead of filing a complaint with HUD or a state agency, the complainant may choose to file a lawsuit directly in federal or state court.

An individual who is subjected to illegal housing discrimination is generally entitled to recover damages, which may include one or more of the following:

1. Monetary compensation for actual damages, including reimbursement for expenses incurred in seeking alternative housing;

2. The right to obtain the desired housing;

3. Any other damages suffered which are provable; and

4. Legal fees and costs.

Victims of housing discrimination may obtain further information and assistance by contacting HUD. In addition, many jurisdictions have their own local fair housing organizations and consumer protection agencies that can be a source of further information. Legal aid organizations may also provide free advice and/or representation to persons who qualify for services. There are also private attorneys who specialize in housing discrimination litigation.

As further discussed below, HUD enforces the federal *Fair Housing Act*, which prohibits discrimination based on race, color, national origin, religion, sex, family status, or disability. Nevertheless, the Federal *Fair Housing Act* provisions do not replace any state or local laws that provide greater protection.

A directory of HUD Fair Housing Enforcement Centers is set forth at Appendix 4 of this almanac.

THE FEDERAL *FAIR HOUSING ACT*

The *Fair Housing Act* prohibits housing discrimination based on one's race, color, national origin, religion, sex, family status, or disability, and provides that no one may take any of the following actions if based on these factors:

1. Refuse to rent or sell housing;

2. Refuse to negotiate for housing;

3. Make housing unavailable;

4. Deny a dwelling;

5. Set different terms, conditions or privileges for sale or rental of a dwelling;

6. Provide different housing services or facilities;

7. Falsely deny that housing is available for inspection, sale, or rental;

8. For profit, persuade owners to sell or rent, an activity known as blockbusting;

9. Deny anyone access to, or membership in, a facility or service related to the sale or rental of housing;

10. Threaten, coerce, intimidate or interfere with anyone who is exercising a fair housing right, or assisting others who exercise that right; or

11. Advertise or make any statement that indicates a limitation or preference based on race, color, national origin, religion, gender, familial status, or handicap.

The *Fair Housing Act* is set forth at Appendix 5 of this almanac.

ADDITIONAL PROVISIONS RELATED TO DISABLED PERSONS

If an individual, or someone associated with the individual, has a physical or mental disability that substantially limits one or more major life activities, and has a record of such a disability or is regarded as having such a disability, a landlord may not:

1. Refuse to let the tenant make reasonable modifications to the dwelling or common use areas, at the tenant's own expense, if necessary, for the disabled person to use the housing.

2. Refuse to make reasonable accommodations in rules, policies, practices or services if necessary for the disabled person to use the housing.

For the purposes of the *Fair Housing Act*, a covered disability may include hearing, mobility and visual impairments, chronic alcoholism, chronic mental illness, AIDS, AIDS Related Complex and mental retardation. Nevertheless, housing need not be made available to a person who is a direct threat to the health or safety of others or who currently uses illegal drugs.

For buildings that were ready for first occupancy after March 13, 1991, and which have an elevator and four or more units, the following provisions apply:

1. The public and common areas must be accessible to persons with disabilities;

2. The doors and hallways must be wide enough for wheelchairs;

3. All units must have:

(a) An accessible route into and through the unit;

(b) Accessible light switches, electrical outlets, thermostats and other environmental controls;

(c) Reinforced bathroom walls to allow later installation of grab bars; and

(d) Kitchens and bathrooms that can be used by people in wheelchairs.

For those buildings that do not have an elevator, the aforementioned standards apply to the ground floor units.

The landlord is also required by law to permit a disabled tenant to make reasonable modifications to the rental property to the extent necessary for the tenant to have what is known as "full enjoyment of the premises." The tenant, however, is generally required to pay the costs for any such modifications. Further, the tenant may be required to restore the rental property to its prior condition when the tenant moves out.

FEDERAL *FAIR HOUSING LAW* EXEMPTIONS

Under certain circumstances, the following properties may be exempt from the federal law:

Small/Owner-Occupied Properties

This exemption generally applies to residential property that is owned by "mom and pop" landlords—e.g., individuals who own three single family homes or less at any one time—or owner-occupied buildings that have four units or less where the owner resides in one of the units.

Religious Organizations and Private Clubs

A restriction on the sale or rental of property owned by religious organizations and private clubs may be limited to their members, if they meet the federal guidelines. Anyone who seeks to use this exception to the *Fair Housing Law* should confirm it with competent legal counsel first, as an error in interpretation could prove costly.

Senior Citizen Housing

A landlord can only discriminate against tenants with children if:

1. The HUD Secretary has determined that it is specifically designed for and occupied by elderly persons under a Federal, State or local government program;

2. It is occupied solely by persons who are 62 or older; or

3. It houses at least one person who is 55 or older in at least 80 percent of the occupied units, and adheres to a policy that demonstrates an intent to house persons who are 55 or older.

Nevertheless, property owners who are otherwise exempt from the law must still comply with the prohibitions against discrimination in advertising. As it relates to senior citizen housing, the advertising is permitted to state that the building does not allow children, or that it is an "Over 55" building, however, the advertising cannot discriminate against other protected classes under the *Fair Housing Law*.

FILING A HUD COMPLAINT

If you think a landlord has broken a federal fair housing law, you can file a fair housing complaint with HUD's Fair Housing Enforcement Center. Complaints must be filed within one year of the alleged discriminatory act. If HUD determines that your state or local agency has the same fair housing powers as HUD, it will refer your complaint to that agency for investigation. You will be notified of the referral. That agency must begin work on your complaint within 30 days or HUD may reclaim the complaint.

When filing a complaint with HUD, be prepared to give the following information:

1. Your name and address;

2. The name and address of the person you claim violated the law;

3. The address of the rental property;

4. The date when the incident occurred; and

5. A short description of the circumstances.

HUD will notify you when it receives your complaint. HUD will also notify the alleged violator—called the "respondent"—and permit that person to submit an answer to the complaint. HUD will then investigate your allegations, and determine whether there is reasonable cause to believe the *Fair Housing Act* has been violated.

HUD will then normally appoint a mediator to negotiate with the landlord and reach a settlement, also known as a "conciliation." A conciliation agreement must protect both you and the public interest. If an agreement is reached, HUD will take no further action on your complaint unless it has reasonable cause to believe that the conciliation agreement is breached. In that case, HUD will generally recommend that the Attorney General file suit.

If HUD is unable to negotiate a settlement, an administrative hearing may be held to determine whether discrimination has occurred. If the case does proceed to an administrative hearing, HUD attorneys will litigate the case on your behalf. An Administrative Law Judge (ALJ) will consider your evidence and any evidence provided by the respondent landlord. If the ALJ decides that discrimination has occurred, the ALJ may order the landlord to:

1. Pay compensation for actual damages, including humiliation, pain and suffering;

2. Provide injunctive or other equitable relief, e.g., make the housing available;

3. Pay the Federal Government a civil penalty to vindicate the public interest. The maximum penalties are $10,000 for a first violation and $50,000 for a third violation within seven years; and/or

4. Pay reasonable attorney's fees and costs.

If there is noncompliance with the ALJ's order, HUD may seek temporary relief, enforcement of the order or a restraining order in a United States Court of Appeals. In addition, the Attorney General may file a suit in a Federal District Court if there is reasonable cause to believe a pattern or practice of housing discrimination is occurring.

A HUD Fair Housing Discrimination Complaint form is set forth at Appendix 6 of this almanac.

Federal District Court

If either you or the respondent landlord chooses to have the case decided in Federal District Court instead of at an administrative hearing, the Attorney General will file a suit and litigate it on your behalf. Like the ALJ, the District Court can order relief, and award actual damages, attorney's fees and costs. In addition, the court can award punitive damages.

Individual Civil Lawsuit

You are also entitled to file your own individual civil lawsuit in Federal District Court or state court within two years of the alleged violation. This is so even if you already filed a complaint with HUD, provided you have not signed a conciliation agreement, or an ALJ has not started an administrative hearing. If you prevail, the court may award you actual and punitive damages, as well as attorney's fees and costs.

CHAPTER 4:
THE LEASE

IN GENERAL

Prior to renting, the landlord generally requires the prospective tenant to sign a lease—also referred to as a rental agreement. A lease is the contract between the landlord and the tenant that forms the legal basis for the landlord-tenant relationship, and sets forth the rights and obligations of both parties. The lease gives the tenant the right to use and occupy the rental property for a period of time. At the end of the lease term, use and possession of the rental property must be returned to the landlord.

ORAL AND WRITTEN LEASES

A lease can be made orally or in writing. Although most agreements are written, oral agreements are legally binding if for a duration less than one year. If the lease extends beyond one year, most states require that it be in writing. The problem with oral agreements is that there is the risk of future misunderstanding over lease terms, and there is no document to look to when a dispute arises, causing potential problems for enforcement.

Further, the landlord or the tenant can unilaterally terminate the lease at any time, for no reason at all, as long as there is advance written notice. The required notice must coincide with the manner in which rent is paid. For example, if the tenant pays rent every month, the notice must be given one month in advance. If the tenant pays rent every week, the notice must be given one week in advance. In addition, without a written lease, the landlord can raise the rent provided he or she gives the tenant advance written notice as stated above.

The advantage of a written lease is that it sets forth the terms of the tenant's agreement with the landlord, and establishes the term of the lease, during which time the tenancy cannot be terminated unless the tenant violates the lease. In addition, the rent cannot be raised during the term of the written lease unless the lease allows a rent increase.

Nevertheless, the parties to a lease are under a legal duty to deal with each other fairly and in good faith, whether or not the duty is expressed in writing. This means that the parties are to negotiate honestly and in a reasonable manner.

DIFFERENCE BETWEEN A LEASE AND RENTAL AGREEMENT

Although the terms are often used interchangeably, the primary difference between a lease and a rental agreement is the period of occupancy.

Lease

A lease sets forth the total amount of time that the lease will be in effect. During this time, the landlord cannot unilaterally change any of the terms and conditions of the rental, such as raise the rent, unless his or her right to do so is set forth in the lease. This affords a certain measure of protection to the tenant, who has the security of knowing that he or she has a home under a long-term agreement at a set rental amount. Although some leases may contain rental increase provisions, the tenant knows in advance how much of an increase to expect and how often it will be imposed.

Further, the landlord cannot evict a tenant during the lease term, unless for cause, such as non-payment of rent or a violation of a term of the lease which expressly subjects the tenant to eviction. In addition, absent mutual agreement, neither the tenant nor the landlord can end the lease agreement prior to its expiration.

Because the tenant is bound to the lease for its entire period, he or she cannot move, if necessary, without suffering the consequences of breaking the lease. If so, the landlord may be able to recover rent for the balance of the lease period, but usually only until another tenant is found.

A tenant can legally move prior to the expiration of the lease if he or she has good cause to do so. This may occur if the landlord fails to make necessary repairs to the rental property that affects the tenant's ability to enjoy the property—a situation known as "construction eviction."

Periodic Rental Agreement

When the parties do not wish to commit to a set period of time to be bound to the rental property, a periodic tenancy arises. In that case, they may execute a periodic rental agreement. A periodic rental agreement generally sets forth the length of time that passes between the tenant's obligation to pay the rent—e.g., month-to-month or week-to-week.

Unlike a lease, the periodic rental agreement does not set forth a time period during which the agreement is binding on the parties. Thus, a periodic rental agreement whereby the tenant is obligated to pay rent every month creates a "month-to-month" tenancy, and one which requires the tenant to pay rent every week is known as a "week-to-week" tenancy.

The tenancy is thus extended or renewed for an additional period of time each time the rental payment is made. As long as the rental payments are made, and the landlord does not request the tenant to move out, the tenant is permitted to continue renting the property. The tenancy is automatically renewed at the end of each period unless the tenant or landlord gives written notice that he or she does not want to continue renting the property.

The amount of time which passes between rental payments determines the required notice a tenant must give the landlord if he or she wishes to move out of the rental property. For example, a month-to-month tenant is generally required to give the landlord at least one month's notice before moving.

In addition, the landlord is likewise obligated to give the tenant the same notice if the landlord no longer wants to rent to the tenant, or if the landlord wishes to raise the rental amount or change any other terms of the rental agreement.

The required notice time cannot be less than the period of time between rental payments unless both the landlord and tenant agree, in writing, to a shorter notice period. In addition, many jurisdictions require a minimum notice period of 30 days, regardless of the period involved or whether there has been a contrary agreement between landlord and tenant. If a periodic rental agreement is undertaken orally—i.e., without any written terms—such an agreement is still legally binding on both the landlord and the tenant.

LEASE PROVISIONS

Many landlords use preprinted form leases which often contain a lot of "legalese" that favors the landlord's position. The prospective tenant should read the entire lease before signing, and make sure he or she understand all of its provisions. If the tenant is unsure about any of the terms in the lease, a legal opinion should be sought. If the lease contains terms that are inapplicable to the particular rental, those clauses are stricken.

Some preprinted form leases contain provisions that are not enforceable in a court of law. Such provisions should be stricken from the lease. Examples of illegal terms include but are not limited to:

1. A provision that waives the tenant's rights under the applicable law;

2. A provision that waives the tenant's right to defend himself in an action by the landlord—e.g., such as an eviction action—or that requires the tenant to pay the landlord's legal fees and costs;

3. A provision which eliminates or limits the landlord's liability under circumstances where he or she would be legally responsible; or

4. A provision giving the landlord unlimited access to the rental property without notice.

Both the landlord and the tenant have the right to change the particular terms and conditions of the pre-printed form insofar as the terms are subject to negotiation. All leases should include any promises made by the landlord to the tenant which are not already part of the form. Any changes to the printed form must be made in writing and acknowledged by both parties. Any terms that conflict with those changes should be stricken.

If the lease presented is one which is drawn up informally by the landlord, it is still binding on the parties.

The following information is commonly included in a standard lease:

1. The name of the landlord;

2. The name of the tenant;

3. The names of any other persons who will occupy the rental property;

4. The address of the rental property;

5. A description of the rental property, e.g., 2 bedroom/2 bath unit;

6. The term of the rental, e.g., month-to-month, 1 year, 5 years, etc.;

7. The amount of rent that the tenant must pay the landlord;

8. The rent due date;

9. The manner in which it is to be paid, e.g., in person or by mail, etc.;

10. Information regarding the security deposit, e.g., the amount, whether it will be held in an interest-bearing account; and when and it will be returned at the end of the lease;

11. The result of a default of one of the terms of the lease, e.g, if the tenant fails to pay rent or the landlord refuses to make necessary repairs;

12. Whether a late fee will be assessed if rent is not paid on time;

13. Whether the tenant may operate a business out of the rental, assuming local zoning ordinances permit such activities;

14. Whether the tenant will be in default in the event that the tenant disturbs other tenants' "right of quiet enjoyment"

15. The respective duties of the landlord and tenant regarding the maintenance of the rental property;

16. Options available at the end of the term, e.g., option to renew, notice of termination by tenant, etc.

17. Conditions under which the landlord may be permitted to enter the rental property—i.e., right of entry provisions.

18. Whether the tenant will be responsible for paying the attorney fees and costs incurred in a lawsuit, in the event that a lawsuit is filed and the tenant loses;

19. Whether the tenant may have a pet and, if so, what kind and how many;

20. Whether an additional pet deposit will be required;

21. Tenant's rights if there is a building sale during the term; and

22. Sublease and assignment rights.

Two sample leases are set forth at Appendix 7 and Appendix 8 of this almanac.

Once the lease has been signed by both parties, the tenant should request a signed copy for his or her records and future reference.

SPANISH LANGUAGE RENTAL AGREEMENTS

In some states, the law provides that where a Spanish-speaking prospective tenant negotiates with a landlord in the Spanish language, the tenant is generally entitled to receive a written translation of the proposed rental agreement before signing. This is so whether or not the tenant requests such a translation. Failure to do so may result in cancellation of the agreement. Nevertheless, if the tenant negotiated the agreement through a qualified interpreter of his or her own choosing, this requirement may be waived.

DISPUTES

Legal disputes between landlords and tenants are common, and may arise for a number of reasons, such as a disagreement over a rent increase, or who will take responsibility for certain repairs. Litigation is expensive, and should rarely be the parties' first choice for resolving the dispute. Many leases contain an arbitration clause that requires the parties arbitrate or mediate disputes arising under the lease. This method of dispute resolution is less expensive and more expeditious than litigation.

A sample lease arbitration clause is set forth at Appendix 9 of this almanac.

RENT

In addition to other responsibilities, a lease requires the tenant to pay the landlord a specified amount of money on a periodic basis as set forth in the lease. This payment is called rent. For example, a lease may require that rent be paid on a monthly basis by the 15th of each month. Periodic tenancies generally require the rent to be paid at the beginning of each period. For example, a week-to-week tenant may be required to pay rent every Friday, and a month-to-month tenant may be required to pay rent on the 1st of each month.

In order to document that the rent has been paid in case there is a dispute, the tenant should pay by check or money order so they have a receipt. If the tenant pays the rent in cash, he or she must obtain a receipt from the landlord.

A landlord is usually entitled to charge a late fee if rent is not paid on time, according to the lease. Nevertheless, the late fee must be reasonable in amount. Exorbitant late fees will not likely hold up in a court of law. Many leases contain a "grace period"—i.e., a short time period following the due date during which late fees will not be assessed if the rent is received within that time, e.g., 10 days.

In addition, if the tenant pays his or her rent by check, and the check is dishonored by the bank for any reason, the landlord is entitled to a returned check fee. Again, the amount of the fee must be reasonable, e.g., the penalty charged the landlord by his or her bank as a result of the returned check, plus related costs.

In general, rent cannot be increased during the term of the lease unless the lease expressly provides for such an increase. A landlord can raise the rent for a periodic tenant provided the tenant is given advance written notice within the prescribed period of time, e.g., a 30-day notice for a month-to-month tenant and 7-day notice for a week-to-week tenant.

The tenant's duty to pay rent is one of the primary aspects of the landlord-tenant relationship. At common law, a tenant's duty to pay rent continued regardless of whether the landlord breached many or most of the other terms of the agreement. Most jurisdictions have now dispensed with this common-law rule, and hold that a material breach by the landlord of his implied or express obligations relieves the tenant from his or her duty to pay rent until the landlord cures the breach.

For example, if the landlord refuses to make necessary repairs, a tenant generally has the right to withhold the rent and deposit the funds into an escrow account. The tenant may then have the repairs made and deduct the amount of the repairs from the rent. This is a practice known as "repair and deduct."

The tenant's duty to pay rent does not cease if the tenant abandons the property prior to the end of the lease, unless the landlord has violated his or her express or implied duties to make repairs necessary to the enjoyment and habitability of the rental property. In that case, the tenant may legally abandon the rental property under the doctrine of constructive eviction, and the landlord would not be entitled to any additional rent.

Further, if the tenant abandons the rental property, and the landlord takes possession of the property and uses it for his or her own purposes, this implies that the landlord has accepted the tenant's abandonment of the property and also relieves the tenant of the duty to pay any further rent to the landlord.

RENT CONTROL AND STABILIZATION LAWS

Many jurisdictions have laws which prohibit or limit the amount of rent increase a landlord may assess for rental property—a practice generally known as rent control. Although it is not a new concept, rent control became most prevalent during World War II when the federal government began to regulate the prices of goods, services, and residential rent.

Although federal rent control laws expired in 1950, many rental properties are still under rent-control because state laws permit the tenants to keep them in the family down through the generations. The rent for such properties can only be increased by an amount determined by the government.

Rent stabilization laws were first enacted due to a severe shortage of affordable housing. Rent stabilization laws regulate the amount of rental increases, and govern the manner in which leases may be terminated. One and two-family homes are generally exempt from rent stabilization laws.

Because rent control and rent stabilization laws may vary according to the jurisdiction, the reader is advised to check the law of his or her own jurisdiction. For example, some jurisdictions provide that the landlord cannot raise the rent when a new tenant moves into a rent controlled dwelling, while other jurisdictions permit the landlord to increase the rent of a newly vacant apartment to the fair market price.

ALTERATIONS AND MODIFICATIONS TO RENTAL PROPERTY

Tenants often choose to alter or modify the rental property, particularly when they have signed a long-term lease. Tenants are entitled to decorate the rental property, however, they sometimes seek to do more than merely redecorate.

In general, courts have held that a tenant is permitted to alter rental property if "reasonably necessary in order for the tenant to use the leased property in a manner that is reasonable under all the circumstances." For example, it may be reasonable for a tenant to put up a fence around the property if he or she has a dog on the premises. Nevertheless, the landlord still has the right to demand that the tenant restore the property to its original condition prior to the expiration of the lease.

Under some circumstances, the landlord may be able to prevent the tenant from removing a fixture from the rental property. A fixture is an item of personal property—known as "chattel"—which the tenant permanently attaches to the property. The ease of the item's removal and replacement will usually govern whether or not the tenant can remove it when he or she leaves.

For example, the tenant may have the right to remove a ceiling fan because it is relatively easy to detach and replace with a standard light fixture. However, if the tenant installed a decorative sink and vanity in the bathroom, it will most likely have to remain. If removing the fixture would in some way negatively affect the landlord's interest in the property, or would prevent the property from being restored to its original condition, the courts have generally held that the fixture must remain.

SALE OF RENTAL PROPERTY

If the landlord sells the rental property prior to the end of the lease term, the tenant maintains the right to live in the rental property until the lease expires, under the same terms and conditions. In addition, the tenant maintains his or her right to have the security deposit refunded at the end of the lease term. Nevertheless, a periodic tenancy can be terminated at anytime upon the required written notice.

If the landlord defaults on the mortgage and the mortgage company forecloses on the loan, the tenant is also entitled to remain in the rental property until the end of the lease. The tenant should send a notice to the mortgage company with a copy of the lease stating his or her right to remain in the rental property. The letter should be sent by certified mail, return receipt requested, so there will be proof of notice of the tenant's intent to continue to occupy the rental property.

THE LANDLORD'S RIGHT OF ENTRY

A tenant is entitled to privacy, exclusive possession, and the right to "quiet enjoyment" of the rental property. Thus, a landlord's right of entry is limited. In general, a landlord can only enter the rental property under the following circumstances:

1. In case of an emergency;

2. To make necessary repairs or to assess the need for repairs;

3. To show the property to prospective buyers or tenants; and

4. Upon abandonment of the rental property by the tenant.

Unless there is an emergency, or the tenant has abandoned the premises, the landlord is generally required to give the tenant advance notice—e.g., at least 24 hours—before entering the rental property for any other purpose.

Many states also allow a landlord the right of entry during a tenant's extended absence, in order to maintain the property as needed. However, a landlord may not enter merely to check up on the tenant and the rental property.

In general, you cannot refuse to let the landlord into the apartment without good reason. For example, you can require advance notice, or prevent the landlord from entering the apartment during unusual hours—e.g., in the middle of the night—unless there is an emergency. If you prevent the landlord from entering the apartment without good reason, the landlord may have the right to terminate your lease and start eviction proceedings, or take you to court to obtain a court order allowing the landlord the right to enter the premises.

In addition, you cannot circumvent the landlord's right of entry by changing the locks on the doors. Even if you have the right to change the locks, you are generally required to provide the landlord with a set of keys to the new lock.

SUBLEASES

Under certain circumstances, a tenant may desire to sublet his or her property, e.g., the tenant must temporarily relocate due to a job assignment. A sublease is a rental agreement entered into between the original tenant and a new tenant—known as a subtenant—who moves into the rental property while the original lease is still in effect. The subtenant has the right to use and occupy the rental property leased by the tenant from the landlord.

Even though the tenant no longer lives in the rental property, the tenant usually remains solely obligated under the original lease with the landlord, and is still responsible for payment of the rent, unless all three parties agree to relieve the tenant of this obligation. The tenant also remains responsible for any damages caused by the subtenant. The subtenant becomes responsible for payment of rent to the original tenant, but is not directly obligated to the landlord unless the parties agree.

The sublease between the original tenant and the subtenant should be in writing, contain all essential terms, and be signed by both parties. The rights and responsibilities of the subtenant to the original tenant generally conform to the rights and responsibilities of the original tenant to the landlord. The original tenant cannot give the subtenant any greater rights than he or she has under the original lease. For example, if pets are not allowed in the rental property under the original lease, the sublease cannot permit the subtenant to have a pet on the premises.

In general, a tenant is not allowed to sublet the rental property unless the landlord agrees or the lease allows the tenant to do so. Most leases prohibit subleasing because landlords want to maintain strict control over who occupies the rental property. However, the tenant can seek permission from the landlord to sublet the rental property.

A sample sublease is set forth at Appendix 10 of this almanac.

ASSIGNMENT OF LEASE

An assignment of a lease is similar to a sublease in that it is an agreement between an original tenant and a new tenant which gives the new tenant the right to occupy the rental property. However, an assignment is usually sought under circumstances where the original tenant does not intend to return to the rental property, e.g., the tenant purchases a home while the lease is still in effect.

The major distinction between a sublease and an assignment is that the new tenant becomes directly responsible to the landlord as if he were the original tenant. Nevertheless, the original tenant remains obligated to the landlord under the original lease unless all three parties agree that the original tenant will be relieved of his or her obligations under the lease—known as a "novation." In that case, the new tenant becomes solely responsible to the landlord.

For example, if the original tenant reneges on his or her obligation to pay rent, the original tenant is still liable to the landlord for the rent even though he or she no longer occupies the rental property. However, if there has been a novation, the new tenant is solely responsible for the unpaid rent, and the landlord can no longer go after the original tenant for payment.

APARTMENT-SHARING

Oftentimes, a tenant may desire to take in a roommate to help pay the rent and share living costs if they are financially unable to handle the rent for the apartment on their own. This is a typical arrangement for college students living off-campus. A roommate might be either a joint tenant or a subtenant, depending upon the terms of the lease or rental agreement. Taking in a roommate inevitably raises a number of legal questions, which are further discussed below.

In general, the landlord must be notified if the tenant takes in a roommate provided the lease or rental agreement specifically requires the tenant to do so, or if it limits the number of people permitted to occupy the rental property. However, as a practical matter, it is prudent to notify the landlord in any event, so as to avoid a conflict with the landlord that may lead to eviction, particularly where there is a periodic tenancy.

The roommate is not a tenant and thus generally has no legal rights or responsibilities in terms of his or her relationship with the landlord. However, the roommate may take on tenant status if:

1. All parties sign a new lease that includes the roommate as a tenant of the rental property;

2. The parties orally agree to a landlord-tenant relationship; or

3. The roommate pays rent directly to the landlord and the landlord accepts the rent, thus creating a contract implied by the conduct of the parties.

However, if the roommate does take on legal status as a tenant, it should be noted that both the roommate and the tenant will be legally obligated to the landlord for the entirety of the rent, not just one-half. Thus, if one of the parties does not pay the rent, the landlord can recover all of the rent from the other party.

In addition, both parties would be liable to the landlord for the entire cost of any damages sustained to the property. Of course, both tenants have the right to sue each other to recover monies paid on the other's behalf; however, this may prove a difficult, time-consuming, and costly endeavor.

In any event, whether or not the roommate takes on tenant status, it is important that the roommate and the original tenant put their agreement in writing as to their legal relationship. Although this agreement is not binding on the landlord, it may become useful if a dispute arises between the tenants. Some basic terms that should be included in the roommate agreement include:

1. The amount each party is obligated to pay for their share of rent, utilities and other costs associated with the rental property;

2. The date and manner in which such payment shall be made; and

3. The roommate's rights in case the original tenant no longer wants to share the rental property, e.g., notice requirements, etc.

Choosing a roommate to share your apartment should be made carefully. Don't pick an opposite—i.e., if you are neat, don't pick a sloppy person to share the apartment. It is advisable to pick someone who is compatible with your personality and way of life.

Areas you should explore when interviewing a prospective roommate include financial responsibility; political beliefs; privacy; entertaining; personal habits such as smoking and alcohol use, etc. In addition, you should require your prospective roommate to provide you with references, and you should contact those references before entering into any agreement.

"NO-PET" CLAUSES

When you own your own home, nobody can tell you whether or not you can own a pet. But when you rent, it's a whole different story. For a variety of reasons, many landlords simply do not want tenants to have pets living in their rental property, and you generally must abide by any no-pet clause contained in your lease. Most landlords overlook small pets, such as fish, birds, hamsters, etc., and some will even make an exception for cats and small dogs.

No-pet clauses are usually enforced against dogs and, unfortunately, this is one of the biggest reasons many pet owners give for surrendering their canine companions to animal shelters. Irresponsible pet ownership—e.g., owners who let their dogs damage property, bark incessantly at all hours, and intimidate tenants—is a big reason that landlords have instituted no-pet clauses in their lease. Landlords do not want to have to repair damage, listen to complaints from other tenants, or risk liability if a tenant's dog bites someone on the landlord's property.

Even if your lease contains a pet restriction, you may be able to negotiate the no-pet clause with your landlord if you can demonstrate that your dog is well-behaved, and you are a responsible pet owner. You will likely, however, have to agree to certain additional provisions in your lease that address the landlord's valid concerns, and provide proof that your dog won't misbehave. For example, your landlord may require you to repair any damage caused by your dog, or to pay an additional deposit or higher rent in order to offset any damages your pet may cause.

Your landlord may also allow you to keep the dog you presently own, but refuse to allow you to bring in any replacement pets in the future. In addition, the landlord may require you to carry some type of liability insurance in case your dog bites someone, and indemnify the landlord for any damages awarded in a personal injury lawsuit.

If your pet lived with you at your previous residences, it would strengthen your case if you provide your new landlord with letters from your previous landlords and/or neighbors attesting to the fact that your pet never caused any problems. You should also provide proof that your dog is properly licensed and vaccinated. If your dog has had any special training, such as obedience school, provide the landlord with copies of his or her certificate. Offer to bring your dog with you so the landlord can observe the animal's behavior. You can take this opportunity to demonstrate your dog's ability to follow your commands. This is when obedience training comes in handy.

If you are successful in convincing your landlord that your dog will not cause any problems, and your landlord agrees to allow you to keep your pet, make sure you get a waiver of the no-pet clause put in your lease in case the landlord tries to change his or her mind after you have moved into your new home, or sells the rental property to another owner who may want to strictly enforce the no-pet clause.

If all efforts at negotiation have failed, and you are adamant about living in rental property that contains a no-pet clause in your lease, you may be able to obtain a court order allowing you to keep your pet if you can demonstrate that circumstances exist making the restriction unenforceable. Nevertheless, a tenant is not advised to acquire a pet if he or she knows this is a violation of the lease.

Security Concerns

If you can prove you need your pet for security reasons, you may be able to argue that you are entitled to a waiver of the no-pet clause. This argument may prevail if the property is in a high crime area, the landlord has not taken the proper safety precautions to secure the building, and you contend that you need the dog for protection.

Estoppel

A landlord cannot add a no-pet clause to your lease after you have already signed your lease. In addition, if the landlord told you that you could keep your dog, you may be able to challenge an eviction based on the owner's acquiescence. Further, if your pet has been living with you openly and with the knowledge of the landlord for a certain period of time and the landlord did not try to enforce the no-pet clause of the lease, a court may allow you to keep your pet.

Under the estoppel doctrine, the landlord may not be permitted to exercise a no-pet clause at a later date on the basis that he implicitly approved by failing to take steps to enforce the clause, thus waiving his claim by his inaction.

Special Provisions for the Elderly and Disabled

Another scenario in which a no-pet clause may be unenforceable concerns trained assistance dogs, such as seeing eye dogs owned by disabled tenants, and companion animals owned by senior citizens. Numerous studies have shown that pets can be extremely beneficial to the health of the aging population, leading to lower blood pressure, increased motor skills, and mental stimulation.

Applicable Law

Whether or not a tenant will be permitted to keep a pet despite the landlord's "no pet" policy depends in large part on the law which governs the specific problem. A tenant's rights may be regulated by federal, state or local laws. Federal law applies to everyone in the United States and the violation of a federal law is illegal in every state. Federal law determines the minimum protection available to a tenant in rental housing and generally concerns a tenant's civil rights in housing, such as a prohibition against discriminatory practices. State law can provide further specific protections for tenants under the state constitution and statutes enacted by the state legislature however state law cannot provide a tenant with less protection than the federal law requires. Municipal and local laws provide even more specific regulations.

Federal Law

In recognition of the medical benefits discussed above, elderly and disabled tenants in federally-subsidized housing are allowed to own pets, and landlords must make reasonable accommodations for their disabled tenants. A reasonable accommodation may include allowing a disabled tenant to keep a pet provided it does not cause an undue hardship on the landlord. There are four federal laws that may impact an elderly or disabled tenant's right to keep a companion animal in rental housing.

The *Housing and Urban Rural Recovery Act of 1983*

Under The *Housing and Urban Rural Recovery Act*, the owner or manager of any federally assisted rental housing that is designated for the elderly or disabled cannot prohibit a tenant from keeping a common household pet.

The Act provides that:

> No owner or manager of any federally assisted rental housing for the elderly or handicapped may—
>
> (1) as a condition of tenancy or otherwise, prohibit or prevent any tenant in such housing from owning common household pets or having common household pets living in the dwelling accommodations of such tenant in such housing; or
>
> (2) restrict or discriminate against any such person in connection with admission to, or continued occupancy of, such housing by reason of the ownership of such pets by, or the presence of such pets in the dwelling accommodations of, such person.

Nevertheless, the statute does permit a landlord to remove an animal who is considered a threat or nuisance to others, thus the owner of a companion animal in such rental housing should make a special effort to ensure that their pet behaves appropriately and receives proper care.

In that connection, the Act provides that:

> Nothing in this section may be construed to prohibit any owner or manager of federally assisted rental housing for the elderly or handicapped, or any local housing authority or other appropriate authority of the community where such housing is located, from requiring the removal of any such housing of any pet whose conduct or condition is duly determined to constitute a nuisance or a threat to the health or safety of the other occupants of such housing or of other persons in the community where such housing is located.

The *Fair Housing Amendments Act of 1988*

Under The *Fair Housing Amendments Act*, it is illegal to refuse to sell or rent a dwelling to a person because of race, color, religion, sex, familial status, or national origin. These prohibitions against discrimination form the basis for permitting persons with disabilities to keep a companion animal in their home when the animal is needed to provide assistance to the disabled tenant. For example, a landlord cannot refuse to rent to, or evict, a blind person because they own a seeing eye dog. Further, the law applies whether or not the disabled individual is the person named on the lease provided the disabled individual is legally living in the dwelling.

The *Fair Housing Amendments Act* applies to nearly all housing, whether the dwelling is for sale or rent, but generally excludes (i) buildings with four or fewer units if the landlord lives in the building; and (ii) private owners who own fewer than three single family homes.

The *Americans With Disabilities Act of 1990*

The *Americans With Disabilities Act* (ADA) also requires public agencies, or agencies receiving federal funds, to provide access for all individuals, regardless of disability. Disabled individuals who need their companion animal as part of their care, treatment or rehabilitation may also rely on this statute as a basis for keeping their pet in their rental home.

The *Rehabilitation Act of 1973*

The *Rehabilitation Act*—the predecessor to the ADA—provides similar protection to disabled persons when the landlord is connected with a federally funded program.

State and Local Laws

Some state and local laws provide the same protection to elderly and disabled tenants living in private housing concerning the right to keep companion animals. However, as set forth above, state and local laws can provide its citizens greater rights than those provided under federal law, but their protections cannot fall below the minimum federal standards. For example, a state may pass laws that give greater protection to the elderly or disabled, much like the federal legislation described above, but cannot place limitations on the protections afforded under the federal law.

CHAPTER 5:
SECURITY DEPOSITS

WHAT IS A SECURITY DEPOSIT?

A security deposit is a fee, in addition to the first month's rent, which the landlord requires the tenant to pay before moving into the rental property. The purpose of the security deposit is to protect the landlord in case the tenant damages the property during occupancy, or if the tenant moves out without paying the rent.

A landlord is usually limited by law as to the amount of security deposit he can require the tenant to pay. Usually, the security deposit is equal to one month's rent. The lease should set forth the amount of security deposit paid, and the circumstances under which the tenant would forfeit all or part of the security deposit. In addition, the landlord must give the tenant advance written notice of any increase in the security deposit, if authorized by the lease.

State laws require the landlord to hold the tenant's security deposit in a bank account, and the tenant must be given information concerning the name of the bank where the funds are being held. Interest earned on the funds generally belongs to the landlord unless there is a written agreement to the contrary, or if the applicable law requires the interest to be turned over to the tenant.

INSPECTION

Many leases contain a provision that prohibits the tenant from "committing waste" in the rental property. This basically means that the tenant has the duty to keep the rental property clean, and shall not intentionally or negligently cause damage to the property.

The tenant is generally entitled to be present when the landlord inspects the property for damage prior to moving out. This is when the tenant's inventory and pre-rental photos or videotape are most useful. If the landlord tries to hold the tenant liable for any conditions that were in existence prior to the tenant's occupancy, the tenant has written and photographic proof to defend his or her position. If a dispute arises over the security deposit, a tenant may sue the landlord to recover the deposit. Some jurisdictions also award a tenant additional damages and legal fees if they prevail in their lawsuit.

In order to maximize your chances of having your security deposit returned in full, in preparation for the inspection, you should clean the apartment thoroughly, repair any damage you caused, and take pictures of the apartment to demonstrate its condition in case you end up in court with the landlord. In addition, after the apartment inspection, you should ask the landlord to sign and date a statement verifying the condition of the apartment at the time the inspection was undertaken.

SECURITY DEPOSIT DEDUCTIONS

Landlords are permitted to make deductions from the tenant's security deposit if the rental property is damaged or excessively dirty, however, deductions cannot be made for reasonable and ordinary wear and tear.

Basically, a landlord may charge a tenant for repairs that are necessary to restore the rental property to the condition it was in when the tenant took possession. The landlord may also charge a tenant for cleaning if it is determined that the rental property was left in an excessively dirty condition, although such a determination is somewhat subjective and may lead to a dispute with the landlord that ends up in small claims court.

REFUND OF THE SECURITY DEPOSIT

If the tenant damages the property or leaves without paying all of the rent due under the lease, the landlord is entitled to keep all or part of the security deposit. Some landlords require a tenant to pay the last month's rent in advance, in addition to the security deposit, as additional protection against a tenant who abandons the property without paying the rent due. The tenant is usually not permitted to apply the security deposit towards rent unless the landlord agrees. Thus, the tenant is required to pay the last month's rent to avoid defaulting on the lease.

If a tenant reaches an agreement with the landlord permitting the tenant to apply the security deposit towards rent, the agreement should be in writing. Insofar as a security deposit is not considered rent, a tenant may get evicted if they treat the security deposit like rent without the landlord's written permission.

If a tenant moves out without owing any rent, and without causing any damage to the rental property above normal wear and tear, he or she is entitled to a refund of the entire security deposit. Many states require landlords to provide the tenant with a detailed list of all deductions taken from a security deposit, whether for unpaid rent or for repairs.

The balance of the security deposit, after the deductions are made, is then returned to the tenant, usually within a prescribed period of time. In most states, the security deposit must be returned within 14 to 30 days after the tenant vacates the apartment. Depending on the state, if the landlord does not send the refund and/or a statement of deductions to the tenant within the applicable time period, the landlord may not be entitled to keep any portion of the security deposit.

A table of state rules for returning security deposits is set forth at Appendix 11 of this almanac.

SUBLEASES AND SECURITY DEPOSITS

If the original tenant sublets the rental property, the landlord is entitled to retain the original tenant's security deposit until the end of the lease. If the tenant needs the money before the lease ends, he or she can ask the landlord to return the security deposit and obtain a substitute security deposit from the subtenant, however, the landlord is not obligated to do so.

The only other option for a refund of the security deposit would be for the tenant to collect a security deposit from the subtenant. Nevertheless, the landlord cannot keep a security deposit from both the original tenant and the subtenant if the total amount exceeds the amount of security deposit required by the lease.

CHAPTER 6:
HEALTH, SAFETY AND HABITABILITY

THE WARRANTY OF HABITABILITY

At common law, a landlord had no general duty to make repairs and keep the rental property in good working order. In fact, the tenant had the implied duty to make minor repairs to the property, although the tenant was not required to undertake major repairs. Tenants have made a lot of progress over the last several decades in gaining greater rights in this area. The warranty of habitability doctrine has now shifted the burden of making repairs from the tenant to the landlord, including minor repairs. This warranty may be either expressed in writing, or implied as an element of the landlord-tenant relationship.

Although some leases still contain a clause which imposes a duty to repair on the tenant, most courts have chosen not to enforce such repair clauses. In addition, clauses which attempt to waive the warranty of habitability have been held invalid as contrary to public policy. A tenant is required to take reasonable care of the rental property, and is generally responsible for damages caused by the tenant, the tenant's guests or the tenant's pets.

Under the warranty of habitability, it is generally required that the landlord ensure, before renting, that the property is habitable—i.e., fit for occupation by humans—and in substantial compliance with building and health codes. In addition, landlords are generally required to maintain the rental property in a habitable condition during the rental period. Minor code violations not affecting habitability, or the failure to undertake minor repairs or cosmetic alterations would not likely violate the implied warranty of habitability.

The sample warranty of habitability clause as codified by New York State is set forth at Appendix 12 of this almanac.

Common defects which may render rental property uninhabitable include but are not limited to:

1. Lack of weather protection, such as broken windows and leaking rooftops;

2. Failure to provide adequate plumbing facilities, including hot and cold running water;

3. Failure to provide an adequate sewage disposal system;

4. Failure to provide adequate heat;

5. Failure to provide adequate lighting;

6. Failure to provide a working stove and refrigerator; and

7. Failure to keep the building clean and free from trash and infestation.

If the landlord neglects the responsibility to maintain the rental property, the tenant should put the landlord on written notice of his or her duty to do so. The letter should detail the repairs that need to be made. In addition, the tenant should take photographs of any visible damage. The tenant should keep one copy of the letter and mail the original to the landlord by certified mail with a return receipt to establish that the landlord received the letter. If after a reasonable period of time the landlord still neglects to make the repairs, there are several courses of action the tenant may take, as discussed below.

Repair and Deduct

Under the "repair and deduct" method, the tenant deducts the amount of money necessary to complete the repairs from his or her rent payment. In order to justify using this remedy, the tenant should only make repairs that breach the warranty of habitability or otherwise threaten the tenant's health and safety.

It is important to keep all repair receipts to justify the amount deducted from the rent. In addition, the tenant should send written notice to the landlord, by certified mail-return receipt requested, explaining his or her reasons for deducting the repair money from the rent.

The tenant runs the risk of a lawsuit by the landlord for nonpayment of rent or eviction, and should be prepared to defend his or her right to deduct the repair money from the rent. Nevertheless, the landlord is generally prohibited from taking any action that may be deemed retaliatory.

Rent Withholding

A tenant may choose to withhold all or part of the rent if the landlord refuses to undertake the necessary repairs. Again, the repairs must be serious enough to render the property uninhabitable or threaten the tenant's health and safety. Under this remedy, the rent is not paid until the landlord makes the necessary repairs. The withheld rent should be maintained in an account. The landlord should be advised, in writing, that the rent money is being held in escrow until the repairs are made.

As with the "repair and deduct" remedy above, rent withholding also subjects the tenant to the risk that the landlord will sue for nonpayment of rent or eviction.

Abandonment and Constructive Eviction

A tenant is generally entitled to abandon the rental property without penalty if it is rendered uninhabitable due to the landlord's failure to make necessary repairs. When rental property is uninhabitable, it creates a condition known as "constructive eviction"—i.e., the condition of the property is such that the tenant is unable to enjoy full use and possession and has thus, as a practical matter, been "evicted" from the property. However, to be constructively evicted, the defects must be serious enough to breach the warranty of habitability or otherwise render the rental property unsafe or unhealthy.

If the tenant must abandon the property under these circumstances, he or she is no longer liable for rent under the lease, and is still entitled to a refund of the security deposit. The tenant should send written notice to the landlord, by certified mail-return receipt requested, explaining his or her reasons for moving.

Renting Property Subject to Condemnation or Housing Code Violations

A landlord is prohibited from renting property which has been condemned, or otherwise rendered uninhabitable due to housing code violations. Housing codes set forth minimally acceptable housing standards, which have long been criticized as being too low. Although housing codes vary according to jurisdiction, these codes generally govern such conditions such as plumbing, heat and hot water, electricity, structural integrity, trash removal, and pest control.

Housing codes were established to ensure that residential rental units were habitable at the time of rental and during the tenancy. Depending on the state, housing code violations may lead to administrative action or to the tenant being allowed to withhold rent.

Arbitration and Litigation

The landlord and tenant may resort to arbitration or mediation to resolve disputes, including those concerning the condition of the rental property. If alternative dispute resolution fails, the tenant's final option would be to file a lawsuit against the landlord for breach of the warranty of habitability.

If the tenant prevails in a lawsuit, the court may award the tenant any actual damages incurred—such as the cost of alternative lodging—and order the landlord to make the necessary repairs. The tenant may also be able to recover legal fees and costs. Punitive damages may also be assessed if it is found that the landlord's actions were intentional.

A sample complaint for breach of warranty of habitability is set forth at Appendix 13 of this almanac.

THE COVENANT OF QUIET ENJOYMENT

As discussed in Chapter 4, the covenant of quiet enjoyment is a guarantee to the tenant that he or she is entitled to use the rental property for his or her own enjoyment, without interference by the landlord. If the landlord obstructs or interferes with the tenant's use of the rental property, this would constitute a breach of the covenant.

As discussed in Chapter 4, a landlord cannot enter a tenant's apartment at unreasonable hours, or without advance notice, unless there is an emergency, even though the lease provides the landlord with the right of entry. In addition, as set forth above, the landlord is required to make necessary repairs to make sure the rental property is safe and habitable. If the landlord fails to make necessary repairs that threaten the tenant's health and safety and impinge upon the tenant's ability to occupy the premises, this failure may also constitute a breach of the covenant of quiet enjoyment. Nevertheless, the covenant is not breached where the landlord's actions are not serious enough to trigger this clause.

Co-Tenants

Further, the landlord is generally not responsible for the actions of the co-tenants living on the rental property unless the landlord either expressly or impliedly authorized any action by a co-tenant which would intrude upon the another tenant's quiet enjoyment of the property. For example, the landlord is generally not responsible because a tenant in the apartment building plays loud music at all hours of the day and night, disturbing neighboring tenants.

If a tenant has a problem with a co-tenant living on the rental property, and the tenant cannot get the offending tenant to cooperate, e.g., by playing music at a reasonable level and during reasonable hours of the day, the tenant should file a written complaint with the landlord. If a number of tenants join in the complaint, the landlord will likely advise the offending tenant to quiet down or face eviction. If the landlord fails to take any action to reduce the noise or other problem after being put on notice, he or she may then be held liable for a breach of the covenant of quiet enjoyment of the leased premises.

A sample covenant of quiet enjoyment of leased premises clause is set forth at Appendix 14 of this almanac.

ACCIDENTS

A landlord may be liable to the tenant or third parties for injuries caused by dangerous or defective conditions on the rental property. In order to hold the landlord responsible, however, the tenant must be able to prove that the landlord was negligent, and that the landlord's negligence caused an injury. The tenant must be able to show that:

1. The landlord had control over the problem that caused the injury;

2. The accident was foreseeable;

3. Repairing the problem would not have been unreasonably expensive or difficult;

4. A serious injury was the probable consequence of not fixing the problem;

5. The landlord failed to take reasonable steps to avoid the accident;

6. The landlord's failure to repair the problem caused the tenant's accident; and

7. The tenant was genuinely hurt as a result of the landlord's negligence.

For example, if a tenant falls and breaks his ankle on a broken front door step, the landlord will be liable if the tenant can show that:

1. It was the landlord's responsibility to maintain the staircase;

2. An accident of this type was foreseeable;

3. A repair would have been easy or inexpensive;

4. The probable result of a broken step is a serious injury;

5. The landlord failed to take reasonable measures to maintain the steps;

6. The broken step caused his injury; and

7. The victim sustained injuries as a result.

An injured person may file a personal injury lawsuit seeking damages for medical bills, lost earnings, pain and other physical suffering, permanent physical disability and disfigurement and emotional distress.

CRIMINAL ACTIVITIES

Landlords are generally responsible for keeping the rental property safe and secure for tenants and guests—e.g., making sure that doors and windows have proper locks and common areas are well-lit, etc. Most states hold landlords legally responsible to some degree in protecting their tenants from burglars and other criminals, as well as from the criminal actions of co-tenants and employees.

The failure to make a reasonable assessment of the crime potential of the area, and follow up with security measures designed to eliminate or reduce the threat of safety, may subject the landlord to a greater degree of legal liability if a tenant is injured as a result of the landlord's negligence.

Landlords must also be vigilant about tenant crime. For example, the landlord may be held legally responsible for tenants who deal drugs from their apartments, particularly if it can be shown that the landlord was aware of the situation and failed to take any action against the tenant. Landlords must be aware of activities taking place on the rental property, and take swift action if a problem arises.

Landlords must also be careful when hiring employees, such as a superintendent or building manager, because such employees generally have access to the individual rentals. A thorough background check should be undertaken prior to hiring. If a building employee causes injury or property loss to a tenant, the landlord will generally be held liable under the legal doctrine of "respondeat superior," which states that the employer is liable for the acts of the employees.

ENVIRONMENTAL HAZARDS

Lead Poisoning in Children

Lead is extremely detrimental to the health and well-being of children. Studies have found that lead poisoning in children can reduce IQ, cause learning disabilities and impair hearing. Children who have elevated blood lead levels often experience reduced attention spans, are hyperactive and can exhibit behavior problems.

At higher exposures, lead can damage a child's kidneys and central nervous system, and cause anemia, coma, convulsions and even death. Nearly one million American children under age six have blood lead levels high enough to impair their ability to think, concentrate and learn. Studies have also shown that pregnant women poisoned by lead can transfer lead to the developing fetus, resulting in adverse developmental effects.

The *Residential Lead-Based Paint Hazard Reduction Act*

The Residential *Lead-Based Paint Hazard Reduction Act*, commonly known as Title X, was enacted in 1992 to address the serious problem of lead poisoning in children. The Environmental Protection Agency (EPA) is responsible for promulgating the regulations that implement Title X. Title X applies to rental property built before 1978.

Under Title X, a landlord must provide the following information to a prospective tenant before entering into a lease:

1. The landlord must give the tenant an EPA-approved information pamphlet on identifying and controlling lead-based paint hazards ("Protect Your Family From Lead In Your Home" pamphlet).

2. The landlord must disclose any known information concerning lead-based paint or lead-based paint hazards on the property. The landlord must also disclose information such as the location of the lead-based paint and/or lead-based paint hazards, and the condition of the painted surfaces.

3. The landlord must provide any records and reports on lead-based paint and/or lead-based paint hazards that are available to the landlord. For multi-unit buildings, this requirement includes records and reports concerning common areas and other units, when such information was obtained as a result of a building-wide evaluation.

4. The landlord must include an attachment to the lease, or insert language in the lease itself, which includes a Lead Warning Statement and confirms that the landlord has complied with all notification requirements. This attachment is to be provided in the same language used in the rest of the lease. The landlords and tenant must sign and date the attachment.

The landlord must retain a copy of the above disclosures for no less than three years from the commencement date of the lease. If the landlord fails to comply with Title X, he or she faces monetary penalties for each violation and treble damages if a tenant is injured by the owner's willful noncompliance. Additional information on Title X and lead poisoning is available from the National Lead Clearinghouse by telephone at: (800) 424-LEAD, or from the Office of Lead Hazard Control on website: http://www.hud.gov/lea/leahome.html.

Exceptions

Most private housing, public housing, Federally owned housing, and housing receiving Federal assistance are covered by Title X except the following:

1. Housing certified as lead-free by an accredited lead inspector;

2. Lofts, efficiencies and studio apartments;

3. Short-term vacation rentals;

4. A single room rented in a residential dwelling;

5. Retirement communities—i.e., housing designed for seniors where one or more tenants is at least 62 years old—unless children are present.

Radon

Radon is a radioactive gas that is found in soil and rock in all parts of the United States. It is formed by the decay of uranium, which is a natural process. Radon gas is invisible, and it has no odor or taste. Radon may be found in all types of homes and buildings in the United States. If there is radon gas in the ground, it can seep into a building. Radon typically moves up from the ground into a home through drains, cracks or other holes in the foundation. Radon then can be trapped inside the home.

Health Effects of Radon

Studies show that radon is the second leading cause of lung cancer behind cigarette smoking, causing between 7,000 and 30,000 lung cancer deaths each year in the United States. Radon gas decays into radioactive particles that can get trapped in your lungs when you breathe. As they break down, these particles release small bursts of energy. This can damage lung tissue.

The higher the radon level indoors, the greater the amount you breathe. Thus, inhaling indoor air containing radon over a period of many years can increase your risk of getting lung cancer. Your chance of getting lung cancer from radon depends on how much radon is in your home and how much time you spend in your home. If you are a smoker or a former smoker, the risk of getting lung cancer from radon is even greater.

Landlord Liability

As discussed above, the landlord is responsible for making sure the rental property is safe, health and habitable. Thus, they are required to make sure the radon level in the rental property is within acceptable limits. There are steps that rental property owners can take to address the problem of high radon levels.

High radon levels can be reduced by making repairs to the building. The Environmental Protection Agency provides information on ways to fix radon problems. In addition, many states have programs set up to train or certify radon professionals, and can provide referrals. The cost of radon reduction depends on the size and other characteristics of the building.

Tenants who are concerned about radon levels in the rental property can test for radon with a relatively inexpensive radon test device, which can be purchased in a hardware store. The price includes the cost of having the laboratory analyze the test.

A low cost radon test kit may also be purchased from the National Radon Hotline by calling 1-800-SOS-RADON (1-800-767-7236).

Other Environmental Hazards

In addition to lead and radon poisoning, landlords may be liable for tenant health problems caused by exposure to other environmental hazards, such as asbestos. The Occupational Safety and Health Administration (OSHA) has issued strict standards for the testing, maintenance and disclosure of asbestos in buildings constructed before 1981. For further information, OSHA may be reached by telephone at: 1-800-321-OSHA or on their website: http://www.osha.gov.

THE TENANT'S RESPONSIBILITIES FOR REPAIR AND MAINTENANCE

As set forth above, the landlord is required to provide safe and habitable housing and adhere to norms of cleanliness pursuant to a variety of laws and regulations. However, the tenant also has some legal responsibilities in this regard. For example, a tenant cannot go after a landlord for failure to keep the rental property fit and habitable if the tenant's own actions have "contributed substantially" to the habitability problem.

Many states impose the certain requirements on tenants, which generally include the following:

1. The tenant must keep the rental as clean and sanitary as the condition of the premises permits.

2. The tenant must dispose of all rubbish, garbage, and other waste in a clean and sanitary manner.

3. The tenant must properly use and operate all electrical, gas, and plumbing fixtures, and keep them as clean and sanitary as their condition permits.

4. The tenant must not willfully or wantonly destroy, deface, damage, impair, or remove any part of the structure or dwelling unit or the facilities or equipment, nor permit anyone else on the premises to do so.

5. The tenant must use the premises only as it was designed or intended to be used for living, sleeping, cooking, or dining.

In addition, if the tenant causes a serious habitability problem in the rental property—e.g., damages the kitchen sink rendering it inoperable—the tenant is responsible, and the landlord can insist that the tenant pay for the repair.

CHAPTER 7:
RENTER'S INSURANCE

IN GENERAL

Prior to moving into rental property, the tenant is advised to obtain renter's insurance. Renter's insurance refers to an insurance policy, similar to a homeowner's policy, which insures the tenant for property lost as a result of theft, vandalism, fire or other catastrophe. The policy usually assesses a deductible. In case of a loss, the insurance carrier generally pays the tenant for any losses sustained over and above the deductible.

For example, if personal property valued at $1,000 is stolen from the rental property, and the insurance policy has a deductible of $250, the insurance carrier will reimburse the tenant the sum of $750.

A renter's insurance policy may also include personal liability coverage which protects the tenant from lawsuits filed by others, such as a guest who has been injured on the rental property. Renter's insurance pays the other party for their losses, as well as the cost of your legal defense.

LANDLORD'S INSURANCE POLICY

In most cases, the landlord's insurance policy covers only structural damage to the building itself—and many landlord policies don't even go that far if the damage is caused by a tenant. Although most landlords already have insurance that covers the rental property, this does not necessarily protect the tenant from legal liability.

For example, if a tenant negligently causes a fire and destroys the rental property, the landlord may be able to recover his losses from his insurance carrier, however, the insurer may then turn around and seek compensation from the tenant who caused the damage. The tenant would also be liable to any of the other tenants whose possessions were damaged or lost as a result of the fire.

COST

Because the price and type of coverage varies among insurance carriers, the tenant is advised to shop around for the best coverage at the best price. Nevertheless, the cost of renter's insurance is usually quite low compared to the coverage available should a problem arise, not to mention the peace of mind knowing that your prized possessions are protected.

EXTENSION OF COVERAGE

Renter's insurance extends beyond on-premise theft and hazards. For example, if your property is stolen while you are on vacation, you will be covered for the loss. In addition, if an item is stolen from your car, it will also be covered. You are also protected if someone is injured on your property.

PERSONAL PROPERTY

Most people do not believe they have amassed enough possessions to justify obtaining renter's insurance. However, the value of all of the items of personal property one may own often adds up to a significant amount. According to State Farm Insurance Company, most people own more than $20,000 worth of property.

In order to insure your personal property, you should first inventory your possessions by making a list containing the name and description of each item, along with its year of purchase and what you think it would cost to replace it today. Examples of personal property that you should list include:

1. Stereo systems, DVD and VCR players, and television sets
2. CDs, DVDs, videos, and tapes
3. Cameras and other photography equipment
4. Movable appliances, including microwave oven
5. Furniture
6. Sports equipment
7. China and glassware
8. Clothing
9. Books
10. Miscellaneous

The following items may be covered under renter's insurance, with limitations:

1. Property typically covered with limitations:

2. Home computers

3. Cash, including coin collections

4. Checks, traveler's checks, and securities

5. Jewelry and watches

6. Precious and semi-precious stones

7. Comic books, trading cards, and stamps, including collections

8. Antiques and fine art

9. Goldware and silverware (theft)

10. Rugs, wall hangings, and tapestries

11. Firearms

12. Furs or clothing trimmed in fur

13. Boats or other watercraft, and related equipment

NATURAL HAZARDS COVERAGE

Coverage for damages resulting from a natural-hazard varies by state and company, but most policies protect your property against losses created by the following:

1. Vandalism

2. Water damage from failure of plumbing or appliances

3. Frozen water pipes

4. Hail

5. Windstorm

6. Smoke

7. Explosion

8. Vehicles or aircraft

EXTRAORDINARY HAZARDS COVERAGE

For a higher premium, most insurance carriers offer options to add coverage for hazards not included in a standard renter's policy:

1. Earthquake, landslide, or other damage caused by movement of the earth;

2. Water damage cause by an underground source or flooding; and

3. Nuclear-hazard damages.

CHAPTER 8:
LEASE TERMINATION AND EVICTION

MOVING OUT

A tenant who plans to move must determine his or her legal rights to terminate the tenancy according to the type of agreement entered into with the landlord. If the tenant has signed a valid lease for a set period of time, the tenant cannot move before the expiration of the lease term, unless the landlord agrees to break the lease. In the case of a periodic tenancy, neither the landlord nor the tenant are bound by the rental agreement to any set term. Therefore, upon the required advance notice, either party is entitled to end the tenancy.

EXPIRATION OF LEASE TERM

A lease expires automatically when the set term ends, at which time the tenant must vacate the premises. Tenants who wish to renew their lease and extend the term of their tenancy should do so within a reasonable period of time prior to its expiration. Absent a lease provision to the contrary, the landlord is not entitled to notice because the lease expiration date already puts the landlord on notice that the tenant will be vacating the premises on or before a certain date.

A tenant who does not vacate the rental property on or before the lease expiration date—i.e., known as a "holdover" tenant—automatically becomes a periodic tenant if a new lease is not signed and the landlord continues to accept rent. However, if the landlord refuses to accept rent from the holdover tenant, the landlord can begin eviction proceedings, without notice.

As discussed in Chapter 5, prior to moving, the tenant should request the landlord to inspect the rental property in his or her presence so that any disputes concerning the condition of the property can be addressed and resolved. If the landlord and tenant agree that the rental property is in the same condition upon departure as it was when the tenant arrived, excluding normal wear and tear, the tenant is entitled to a refund of the entire security deposit. If, however, the landlord and tenant agree that there are items in need of repair, the landlord is entitled to deduct the cost of such repairs from the tenant's security deposit.

If a tenant moves out of rental property before the lease term expires, he or she is still liable to the landlord for payment of rent until the expiration date. Nevertheless, the landlord is generally required to make reasonable efforts to rent the property. In that case, the tenant would only be liable for the time the property remained unoccupied. In addition, if the landlord does not attempt to re-rent the property, the tenant may be relieved of his or her obligation to pay some or all of the rent owed.

THE PERIODIC TENANCY

A periodic rental agreement does not contain a set term as does a lease. Therefore, to end a periodic rental agreement, the tenant need only serve the required advance notice upon the landlord. The rental agreement may set forth the required notice period. In general, however, advance notice of termination is 30 days for a month-to-month tenancy, and 7 days for a week-to-week tenancy. Because some jurisdictions may have more stringent notice requirements, therefore, the reader is advised to check the law of his or her own jurisdiction.

The tenant should mail the notice to the landlord by certified mail with a return receipt so that there is no dispute over when the landlord received the tenant's notice. The notice should state when the tenant intends to vacate the premises.

A sample notice to landlord of tenant's intention to vacate leased premises is set forth at Appendix 15 of this almanac.

ABANDONMENT OF RENTAL PROPERTY

If a tenant fails to pay rent, and then leaves the rental property without any notice, prior to the expiration of the lease term, the tenant is considered to have "abandoned" the property. If the landlord suspects that the rental property has been abandoned, he or she is entitled to enter the property, remove any belongings left behind by the tenant, and re-take possession of the property.

The landlord is generally required to store any removed property belonging to the tenant for a reasonable period of time. A notice should be mailed to the tenant at the rental property address so that the Post Office can send it to the tenant's forwarding address, if any. The notice should advise the tenant that the abandoned property will be sold if not claimed within a certain time period.

If the property is not claimed after a reasonable period of time, the landlord may sell the property and apply the proceeds to back rent. Nevertheless, prior to any sale, the landlord should make certain that the tenant did, in fact, abandon the property, or risk having to compensate the tenant at some later date.

Under certain circumstances, a tenant is justified in breaking the lease or abandoning the rental property, including but not limited to: (i) the property becomes uninhabitable such that it threatens the health and safety of the tenant; (ii) the property is destroyed, e.g., by fire or other disaster; or (iii) the landlord breaches a material term of the lease.

EVICTION

In General

If a landlord wants to remove a tenant, there are legally prescribed methods which must be followed. The landlord is not entitled to physically remove the tenant and his or her belongings from the rental property, nor can the landlord make living conditions uninhabitable to try and force the tenant to leave. These types of tactics—generally known as "self-help" measures—are illegal and may result in the landlord having to pay the tenant's damages.

The landlord is usually required to serve the tenant with some type of written notice before terminating the tenancy. Where there is a valid lease, the landlord cannot terminate the tenancy unless he or she has just cause to do so, e.g., the tenant violates a term contained in the lease. If the landlord believes that he or she has just cause to evict the tenant, a three-day notice will be served, as further described below.

In the case of a periodic tenancy, because the rental agreement contains no fixed term, in addition to serving a three-day notice for cause, the landlord is entitled to terminate the tenancy at any time, for no cause whatsoever, provided the landlord serves the tenant with the required advance notice of termination.

As discussed below, the termination notice is generally known as a thirty-day notice, since most periodic tenancies are month-to-month agreements. A week-to-week tenancy may only require a seven-day notice. However, some jurisdictions may have more stringent notice requirements, therefore, the reader is advised to check the law of his or her own jurisdiction.

The Three-Day Notice

A landlord may serve a three-day eviction notice on a tenant who breaches his or her lease or rental agreement. The three-day notice must be properly served upon the tenant—i.e., served in a manner prescribed by the applicable law—to be effective. Proper service must be made upon the tenant to be reasonably certain that the tenant is aware of the action being taken, and has an opportunity to respond.

In general, the landlord or someone acting on behalf of the landlord may serve the notice provided he or she is over the age of 18. There are three principal ways service is generally undertaken:

1. Personal Service: Personal service is accomplished by handing the notice to the tenant. If the tenant refuses to take the notice, the server is authorized to leave the notice in the tenant's immediate vicinity after advising the tenant that the notice is being served upon him or her.

2. Substituted Service: Substituted service is accomplished by leaving the notice with "a person of suitable age and discretion" at the tenant's home or place of business. Service is completed when a copy of the notice is also mailed to the tenant at his or her home address.

3. Nail and Mail: Nail and mail service is accomplished by affixing a copy of the notice to the front door of the rental property. Service is completed when a copy of the notice is also mailed to the tenant at his or her home address. This method is generally used when personal service and substituted service have been unsuccessful.

The most common reasons for eviction include but are not limited to: (i) non-payment of rent; (ii) creating a nuisance; (iii) committing illegal activities on the rental property; and (iv) damaging the rental property.

Rent acceleration clauses that cause all the rent to become due if the tenant breaches a provision of the lease are common in both residential and commercial leases.

The three-day notice must advise the tenant of the reason he or she is being evicted. If the three-day notice is due to non-payment of rent, the landlord must specify the amount of rent due.

Three-day notices generally give the tenant the option of either curing the problem or moving. If the notice was served because of non-payment of rent, the tenant may remain in the rental property if he or she pays the arrears within the three-day period. If the rent is not paid until after the three-day period expires, the landlord has the option of either accepting the late payment, or evicting the tenant and demanding a judgment for any past due rent.

If the three-day notice was served for a reason other than non-payment of rent, the notice usually states whether the problem can be corrected. If the tenant wishes to remain in the rental property, he or she must correct the violation within the three-day period, and should notify the landlord immediately that the violation has been rectified.

If the violation is one which cannot be corrected—e.g., the tenant is being evicted because he or she caused substantial damage to the property—the tenant has no recourse but to leave the premises when the three-day period has expired.

Although the notice may be called a "three-day" notice, it does not necessarily expire at the end of the third day. The first day of the "three-day" period begins the day following the day the tenant was served with the notice, and cannot end on a Saturday or Sunday. For example, if the three-day notice was served upon the tenant on Wednesday, the first day of the three-day period is Thursday and the actual third day would fall on a Saturday. Thus, the tenant has an additional two days, until Monday of the following week, to correct the violation.

Nevertheless, the landlord is prohibited by law from evicting a tenant unlawfully. This may occur if the landlord is acting in retaliation against the tenant because of some prior complaint the tenant may have taken against the landlord. If the tenant suspects the landlord's eviction is unlawful or otherwise defensible, he or she is advised to seek legal counsel.

A sample Three-Day Notice to Tenant to Vacate Leased Premises Due to Non-payment of Rent is set forth at Appendix 17 of this almanac.

The Thirty-Day Notice

In addition to termination for cause, a landlord can terminate a periodic tenancy at any time by merely giving the tenant the required notice. In general, notice is usually required 30 days in advance for a month-to-month tenancy, unless the rental agreement provides for a longer or shorter notice period. A thirty-day notice may be served by any of the methods described above, or by certified or registered mail.

If, however, the tenant has violated the rental agreement—e.g., failed to pay rent—the landlord is only required to give the tenant the three-day notice as discussed above.

The thirty-day notice does not have to state the landlord's reasons for ending the tenancy, unless a local law requires it. For example, some rent control and subsidized housing regulations require "just cause" for eviction, even for periodic tenancies.

A periodic tenant who receives a thirty-day notice generally has no legal right to stay in the rental property beyond the thirty days. If this would pose a grave hardship, the tenant should immediately try and work out some alternative arrangement with the landlord. If the landlord grants an extension, make sure it is in writing. If the tenant fails to move after the thirty-day period expires, the landlord has the right to begin an eviction proceeding against the holdover tenant.

THE EVICTION LAWSUIT

If a tenant does not move after the three-day notice for cause expires—or in the case of a periodic tenant, after the expiration of 30 days without cause—the landlord must bring an eviction lawsuit against the tenant, also known as an "unlawful detainer" lawsuit in order to remove the tenant from the rental property.

The landlord, as plaintiff, must file a complaint against the tenant, as defendant, in the appropriate court. Eviction proceedings—also known as summary proceedings—are intended to move swiftly through an otherwise slow-moving judicial system. The tenant's time to respond to the landlord's complaint is relatively short, e.g., five days. Summary eviction statutes commonly allow a landlord to quickly evict a tenant who breaches statutorily specified lease provisions.

In the response, the tenant should set forth any defenses he or she may have, e.g., that the eviction is unlawful because it is in retaliation for some action taken against the landlord, or that the rental property violates the implied warranty of habitability and the tenant was authorized to withhold the rent, etc. It is imperative that the tenant responds to the landlord's complaint because failure to do so may result in a default judgment.

After the tenant's answer has been served and filed, the Court generally holds a hearing at which time both the landlord and tenant present their evidence and make their arguments. If the court rules for the tenant, the landlord may be held liable for the tenant's damages, including legal fees and costs. In addition, the tenant would be entitled to remain in the rental property.

If the landlord prevails, the judge issues an order that the tenant be removed from the rental property. This order is generally carried out by the sheriff. The tenant can voluntarily leave the premises at anytime between issuance of the order and its implementation by the sheriff. The sheriff is authorized to physically remove the tenant and to seize any items left in the rental property. Once the sheriff has executed the order, the landlord is entitled to take possession of the rental property. The judge may also award the tenant a judgment for unpaid rent, legal fees and costs.

A sample 30-day eviction notice is set forth at Appendix 16 of this almanac.

Hotel/Motel Residents

In general, hotel and motel residents who meet certain requirements—e.g., they have lived in the hotel or motel for more than 30 days and have paid all of the related charges by the thirtieth day—have the same legal rights as tenants. If a hotel resident is considered a tenant as opposed to a mere guest, the hotel manager cannot simply lock the individual out of his or her room, but must take formal legal action through the court to evict the occupant.

In addition, the hotel manager cannot prevent a guest from becoming a tenant by requiring the guest to move before the thirty-day period expires. This is unlawful if the proprietor's purpose is to keep the guest from legally becoming a tenant, and violators are subject to civil penalties and legal fees.

Lodgers

In general, the rights of a lodger renting a room in a private house are the same as those of a tenant. However, in the case of a single lodger in a private house with no other lodgers, his or her rights may be more limited. For example, a lodger may be forced to move following written notice, without a formal eviction proceeding. After the notice period has expired, which is usually the same length of time as the rental payment period, e.g., thirty days, the lodger has no further right to remain in the owner's house and may be removed as a trespasser.

Mobile Home Residents

In general, eviction of mobile home residents is subject to the usual eviction procedures required for tenants, although many jurisdictions have statutes specifically addressing the rights of mobile home and recreational park residents. The reader is again advised to check the law of his or her jurisdiction.

ILLEGAL LANDLORD ACTIONS

A landlord is prohibited from trying to make a tenant abandon the rental property, or from retaliating against a tenant who complains or takes legal action against a landlord. If a landlord takes any illegal actions against the tenant, the landlord may be held liable to the tenant for damages, including legal fees and costs. The following landlord actions have been deemed illegal:

SELF-HELP EVICTION

Self-help as a method of eviction is generally restricted. Some states do not even allow it for tenants who have held over after the end of a lease. Thus, a landlord is prohibited from locking a tenant out of the rental property, e.g., by changing the locks. This is so even if the tenant's rent is in arrears. The landlord's only legal recourse is to begin eviction proceedings.

Utility Shutoffs

A landlord is prohibited from shutting off the utilities to a tenant's rental property for any reason. Further, if the landlord intentionally refuses to pay the utility bills so that the service is terminated, this may also constitute an illegal action.

Removing Tenant Property

A landlord is prohibited from removing a tenant's property from the rental property unless the tenant has abandoned the rental. It would be illegal for the landlord to remove a tenant's property for any other reason.

RESIDENTIAL EVICTIONS UNDER THE *BANKRUPTCY ABUSE PREVENTION AND CONSUMER PROTECTION ACT OF 2005*

The *Bankruptcy Abuse Prevention and Consumer Protection Act of 2005* affects the procedures landlords must follow when dealing with a tenant who has filed for bankruptcy. Generally, if a tenant has filed for either Chapter 7 or Chapter 13 bankruptcy and is behind in the rent, becomes unable to pay the rent, or violates another term of the tenancy that would justify a termination, a landlord cannot deliver a termination notice or proceed with an eviction. This prohibition is known as the "automatic stay," and it means that landlords must go to the federal bankruptcy court and ask the judge to "lift"—i.e., remove the stay.

In most cases, the judge will lift the stay within a matter of days and the landlord can proceed with a termination and eviction. Nevertheless, landlords do not have to go to court if a tenant is using illegal drugs or endangering the property, as explained below.

The automatic stay does not apply, however, if the eviction lawsuit is completed and the landlord obtained a judgment for possession before the tenant filed for bankruptcy. In this situation, under the Act, landlords can generally proceed with the eviction without having to go to court and ask for the stay to be lifted.

Depending on the state, under very limited circumstances, a tenant can stop an eviction based upon non-payment of rent even if the landlord obtained a judgment before the tenant filed for bankruptcy. Within 30 days after filing for bankruptcy, the tenant must take the following steps:

1. The tenant must file a statement with the court certifying that state law allows the tenant to avoid eviction by paying the unpaid rent, even after the landlord has won a judgment for possession.

2. The tenant must serve the landlord with this certification.

3. The tenant must deposit with the clerk of the bankruptcy court any rent that would be due 30 days from the date the petition was filed.

4. The tenant must certify to the bankruptcy court that he has paid the back rent; and

5. The tenant must also serve the landlord with this certification.

At any point during the 30-day period, the landlord can file an objection to the tenant's certification. Within 10 days, the court will schedule a hearing. If the judge determines that the tenant's certifications are not true, the court will lift the stay and the landlord can proceed to recover possession of the property.

Exception for Tenant Drug Use and Property Endangerment

If the landlord wishes to evict a tenant who is using illegal drugs or endangering the rental property, and the tenant files for bankruptcy before the landlord obtains a judgment for possession of the property, the landlord can proceed with the eviction without asking the bankruptcy judge to lift the stay by taking the following steps:

1. The landlords must prepare a certification, or sworn statement, that they have begun an unlawful detainer case based on the tenant's use of illegal drugs or endangerment of the property.

2. The certification must state that the activity has happened within the past 30 days.

3. The certification must be filed with the bankruptcy court.

4. The landlord must serve the certification on the tenant.

If the tenant does not file an objection within 15 days of being served, the landlord can proceed with the eviction without asking the court for relief from the automatic stay.

If the tenant objects to the landlord's allegations, the tenant must file a certification with the court challenging the truth of the landlord's certification, and serve a copy on the landlord.

The bankruptcy court will schedule a hearing within 10 days, at which time the tenant must convince the court that the situation the landlord describes did not exist, or has been remedied. If the court rules for the landlord, the landlord may proceed with the eviction, however, if the tenant prevails, the landlord may not proceed with the eviction.

CHAPTER 9:
CO-OP/CONDO CONVERSION

IN GENERAL

Multi-unit dwellings first became popular in high population density areas, such as New York City, because apartment buildings, which are built vertically, take up less space and are better able to house large numbers of people. These first apartment buildings were rental properties, owned by a landlord, who rented each unit for a profit.

A number of factors led to conversion of these rental properties into co-op or condominium buildings. Rent control and stabilization laws discouraged investment in rental housing because it limited the rents that the landlord could charge, leading to deterioration of the housing due to lack of sufficient funds for proper upkeep of the property. These laws caused a financial hardship on landlords who started losing money on their investment in the rental property after inflation caused maintenance costs to skyrocket while rents remained low. The landlord was stuck with a money-losing investment because nobody wanted to buy a building with a negative cash flow.

Instead of trying to sell the entire rental property, landlords began to convert their rental buildings into co-op or condominium properties, and were able to make money by selling the individual units. Tenants of the property were given information in the form of an offering plan regarding their right to purchase their unit at an "insider" price. If a tenant was not interested in purchasing their unit, they were permitted to remain a rental tenant and continue to pay the legal rent pursuant to the rent control or stabilization law, whichever applied to the property.

PRELIMINARY OFFERING PLAN

Before an owner/sponsor may convert a rental property, they must present an offering plan to each tenant and to the designated governmental authority, e.g., the State Attorney General. The preliminary offering plan is merely a prospectus of the proposed conversion. The preliminary offering plan is referred to as a "red herring" because of the bold red lettering on the cover of the plan.

The information contained in the preliminary offering plan is subject to review and may be supplemented or changed as determined by the Attorney General. The owner/sponsor may also change the terms of the offering plan. Until the review is completed, and the final version of the plan is accepted for filing, no sales or advertisements are permitted.

In some states, such as New York, interests in a cooperative, condominium or homeowners' association may not be sold, or even offered for sale, until an offering plan—disclosing all the material facts and complying with all of the laws—has been submitted to, and accepted for filing by the state's Attorney General.

Before accepting the plan for filing, the Attorney General's office reviews the preliminary offering plan and supporting documents submitted by the owner/sponsor to determine whether they have complied with tenant protection laws and whether the plan appears to disclose all of the information required by all applicable laws and regulations.

By accepting the plan for filing, the Attorney General is merely indicating whether the owner/sponsor appears to have complied with the law. Responsibility for full compliance lies with the owner/sponsor. Acceptance does not mean the Attorney General has approved the financial terms, the price, the description of the building's condition or any other aspect of the plan.

INDEPENDENT EVALUATION

While the offering plan is being reviewed, the tenants should make their own independent evaluation of the offering plan. Outside professionals, such as attorneys and engineers, can be hired in order to evaluate the plan and assess the condition of the building. If it turns out that there is a conflict between the information gathered through the independent evaluation, and the information contained in the offering plan, this should be brought to the attention of the Attorney General for further investigation.

ACCEPTANCE OF THE PRELIMINARY OFFERING PLAN

Once the Attorney General's office has finished their review and determines that there has been adequate disclosure, the offering plan is accepted for filing. The owner/sponsor may choose between two methods to convert the building: (a) an eviction plan; and (b) a non-eviction plan. An eviction plan can subsequently be changed to a non-eviction plan if the circumstances dictate, however, a non-eviction plan cannot be changed to an eviction plan.

Eviction Plan

In general, under an eviction plan, a non-purchasing tenant may be evicted from an apartment after a certain period of time. In order for an eviction plan to be in effect, 51% of the tenants in occupancy must sign written purchase agreements on the date the offering plan is accepted for filing. If the owner/sponsor does not obtain the required percentage of purchase agreements within a specified time period following the acceptance date, the conversion plan is considered abandoned, and no new conversion plan may be submitted for at least one year.

Under an eviction plan, non-purchasing tenants may not be evicted for a minimum number of years from the date the eviction plan is declared effective, and eligible senior citizen and disabled tenants may not be evicted at any time, unless they breach their leases. Rent-stabilized tenants whose leases expire less than the minimum number of years after the date the plan is declared effective are entitled to renewals, subject to rent increases authorized by the Rent Stabilization Law, extending the lease to the end of the designated time period. Rent-stabilized tenants whose leases already extend beyond this time period may not be evicted until their leases expire.

During this time period, the tenants must be provided all of the services and facilities required by law without discrimination between purchasing and non-purchasing tenants. In addition, apartments subject to government regulation, such as rent control, continue to be covered by those laws until the tenant moves out or until government regulation of the apartment ends, and tenants that occupy apartments that are not subject to government regulation cannot be charged unconscionable rents. Nevertheless, non-purchasing tenants may be subject to eviction for nonpayment of rent, illegal use or occupancy of the premises, or any breach by the tenant of obligations under the rental agreement.

Non-Eviction Plan

Under a non-eviction plan, non-purchasing tenants may not be evicted for failure to buy their apartments and may continue to occupy them as rental tenants.

Rights of Senior Citizens During Conversion

Senior citizens are usually protected against eviction if they choose not to purchase their apartments. However, to be eligible for this protection, a senior citizen, or his or her spouse, must be renting an apartment in a jurisdiction that has adopted a law offering such protection, and must have reached a certain age—e.g., 62—on the date the plan is accepted for filing by the Attorney General.

In those jurisdictions, the senior citizen must complete a special exemption form and submit it to the owner/sponsor within a certain time period after receiving the final offering plan. Nevertheless, eligible senior citizens have the right to subsequently change their minds and become purchasers, and can purchase at the price offered to other tenants in the building at the time they inform the owner/sponsor of their decision to buy.

As a person exempt from eviction, a senior citizen may stay in the apartment after the building is converted, as long as rent is paid and other obligations are met. The apartment may be sold, in which case the buyer becomes the senior citizen's new landlord, and all of the responsibilities of the previous landlord to maintain the property become the responsibility of the new owner. If the apartment was covered by rent control, rent stabilization before conversion, that law continues to apply after conversion.

Rights of Disabled Persons During Conversion

To be eligible for protection against eviction, a disabled person must satisfy all four of the following conditions as of the date the offering plan is accepted for filing:

1. The tenant or spouse must have an impairment which results from anatomical, physiological or psychological conditions, other than addiction to alcohol, gambling or any controlled substance, which is demonstrable by medically acceptable clinical and laboratory diagnostic techniques; and

2. The impairment must be expected to be permanent; and

3. The impairment must prevent the tenant from engaging in any substantial gainful employment; and

4. The tenant or spouse must elect not to purchase the apartment by completing a special form distributed by the owner/sponsor in the final offering plan. The completed form must be given to the owner/sponsor within a specified number of days from the date the accepted plan was presented to the tenants.

Tenants who first become disabled after the plan is accepted for filing may still qualify as eligible disabled persons, subject to certain legal conditions. They must complete the appropriate forms within a specified number of days following the onset of the disability.

As with senior citizens, eligible disabled persons may stay in the apartment after the building is converted, as long as rent is paid and other obligations are met. The apartment may be sold, in which case the buyer becomes the senior citizen's new landlord, and all of the responsibilities of the previous landlord to maintain the property become the responsibility of the new owner. If the apartment was covered by rent control, rent stabilization before conversion, that law continues to apply after conversion.

The owner/sponsor can dispute the eligibility of a senior citizen or disabled person by informing the Attorney General that he or she disputes the eligibility of a person claiming senior citizen or disabled status. After reviewing all of the relevant documentation, the Attorney General will issue a determination as to the eligibility of the individual in question.

THE FINAL OFFERING PLAN

The final offering plan is referred to as the "black book" because the bold red lettering contained on the preliminary offering plan (the "red herring") is replaced with black lettering indicating the date the final plan was accepted for filing. The final offering plan constitutes the owner/sponsor's offer to sell co-op or condo units on the terms and conditions set forth in the plan. Each tenant receives a copy of the final offering plan.

Conversion is not automatic even if the plan has been accepted. For example, a specified number of apartments must be purchased before the plan can be declared effective and the building actually converted. The owner/sponsor may also choose to abandon the offering plan and continue to operate the building as a rental property.

In general, tenants have the exclusive right to buy their apartments, or the corresponding shares of stock, for a certain period of time after the final offering plan is presented to them. During this time period, the tenant's apartment may not be shown to a prospective buyer unless the tenant has, in writing, waived the right to purchase.

For an additional time period after the exclusive purchase period has expired, tenants facing eviction may still purchase their apartments, but at this time they must purchase on the same terms as non-tenants. If an occupied apartment is sold to an outside purchaser during this time period, the owner/sponsor must notify the tenant who must match the terms of the contract and purchase the apartment within a specified number of days. Tenants of apartments covered by the government regulation, e.g., rental control, also have the right to match an outside offer for purchase of their apartments.

Apartments unsold at the time a plan is declared effective remain the property of the owner/sponsor, who may sell them for whatever the market will bear. Because the law specifies that the conversion plan may only be declared effective after a specified percentage of the tenants of occupied apartments have agreed to purchase, the owner of a building who contemplates submitting a plan for its conversion to co-op or condo ownership might have some incentive to discourage renting vacant apartments. In some jurisdictions, this practice—called "warehousing"—is restricted, and a conversion plan may be rejected by the Attorney General if he finds that excessive warehousing has occurred.

Specifically, if the Attorney General determines that during the five months immediately preceding submission of the preliminary offering plan, the number of vacant apartments has exceeded a specified percentage of the total number of rental units in the building, and if that rate is more than double the "normal" average vacancy rate for the previous calendar years, the plan will not be accepted for filing.

Conversion laws generally prohibit any person from interrupting, discontinuing or interfering with any essential service which substantially disturbs the comfort or peace and quiet of any tenant who uses or occupies an apartment. The tenant, or the Attorney General, may take legal action to stop harassment.

OBTAINING LEGAL REPRESENTATION

The conversion of a rental apartment building to a cooperative or condominium is a technical and complex process. Experience has shown that a tenant whose building is being converted to a co-op or condo may want to consult a lawyer to ensure that his or her rights are being protected. An attorney familiar with the conversion process will be able to explain it completely, and may be retained to represent the tenants in their negotiations with the building owner.

CHAPTER 10:
THE UNIFORM RESIDENTIAL LANDLORD
AND TENANT ACT

IN GENERAL

The *Uniform Residential Landlord and Tenant Act* (URLTA) was drafted by the National Conference of Commissioners on Uniform State Laws (NCCUSL) in 1972. The NCCUSL is a non-profit unincorporated association that consists of commissioners appointed by each state and territory. The purpose of the Commission is to discuss and debate in which areas of law there should be uniformity among the states and to draft acts accordingly.

The results of these discussions are proposed to the states as either model acts or uniform acts. The "uniform laws" are not actual laws, but are recommendations by the Commission as to what the law should be. The "uniform laws" were written for the purpose of reconciling conflicting laws among the states.

The stated purpose of the URLTA is to remove the landlord and tenant relationship from the constraints of property law and establish it on the basis of contract with all concomitant rights and remedies. The URLTA is intended to be fair to all, thus, it favors neither the landlord nor the tenants.

The Uniform Residential Landlord and Tenant Act (URLTA) is set forth at Appendix 18 of this almanac.

BACKGROUND OF THE URLTA

Existing landlord-tenant law in the United States is derived from English common law during the Revolutionary period. The law developed within an agricultural society at a time when doctrines of promissory contract were unrecognized. The landlord-tenant relationship was viewed as conveyance of a leasehold estate, and the covenants of the parties were generally independent.

As society evolved into a modern urban existence, the law became inappropriate for the rental of property, thus, landlord-tenant law has been modified by statute or judicial interpretation. Vital interests of the parties and public under modern urban conditions required the proper maintenance and operation of housing, thus it became necessary to set forth the minimum duties of landlords and tenants.

It was recognized that the duties of repair and maintenance of the dwelling unit should be imposed upon the landlord because, for example, access and repairs to essential systems outside the dwelling unit were beyond the capacity of the tenant. However, the duties of cleanliness and proper use within the dwelling unit were appropriately imposed upon the tenant.

APPLICABILITY

This URLTA applies to landlord-tenant relationships under rental agreements for residential purposes. It does not apply to rental agreements made for commercial, industrial, agricultural or any purpose other than residential.

In addition, the URLTA is not intended to apply where residence is incidental to another primary purpose such as residence in a prison, a hospital or nursing home, a dormitory owned and operated by a college or school, or residence by a landlord's employee such as a custodian, janitor, guard or caretaker rendering service in or about the premises. The URLTA is intended to apply to government or public agencies acting as landlords.

This URLTA does not apply to an individual who occupies the premises pursuant to a contract of sale, although it does apply to someone who occupies the premises as a holder of an option to purchase, as distinguished from a contract of sale. The URLTA also applies to roomers and boarders, but is not intended to apply to transient occupants.

STATE ADOPTIONS

The states do not always adopt a uniform act exactly as written by the Commission. Some states make changes in an effort to improve on the uniform law. The following states have adopted the URLTA in whole or in part:

Alabama

Alaska

Arizona

Connecticut

Florida

Hawaii

Iowa

Kansas

Kentucky

Michigan

Mississippi

Montana

Nebraska

New Mexico

Oklahoma

Oregon

Rhode Island

South Carolina

Tennessee

Virginia

Washington

REMEDIES

The rights and obligations described in the URLTA are enforceable by court action, although it does not set forth the available remedies, which are left to the individual states to devise. Generally, a remedy may be damages awarded in a tort action, specific performance, or equitable relief.

The URLTA gives the courts of states that enact the Act jurisdiction over landlords who violate its provisions. It also provides a method of obtaining personal jurisdiction by service of process upon a public official of the state. In most states, the public official designated to receive service of process is the Secretary of State.

The URLTA makes it possible for courts to deem certain rental agreements, clauses, settlements, or waivers of claims or rights to be unconscionable as a matter of law. The basic test of unconscionability is whether, in light of the background and setting of the rental marketplace, the conditions of the particular parties to the rental agreement, settlement or waiver of right or claim are so one-sided as to be unconscionable under the circumstances existing at the time of the making of the agreement or settlement. Thus, the particular facts involved in each case are of utmost importance since unconscionability may exist in some situations but not in others.

Attorney's fees under the URLTA may be asserted against either the landlord or tenant, however, the right to recover attorney's fees against the tenant must arise under statute, not by contract of the parties.

LEASE PROVISIONS

Following are some of the important provisions contained in the URLTA, as adopted by the various states.

Lease Term

Under the URLTA, if a rental agreement does not set forth a definite term of lease, the tenant is deemed to have a month-to-month tenancy, regardless of whether the rent is paid weekly, monthly, or in some other manner. In addition, a roomer who pays rent for longer intervals than week-to-week is also deemed to have a month-to-month tenancy.

Maintenance and Repairs

The URLTA reaffirms the obligation of the landlord to maintain the rental property in a fit and habitable condition, and requires disclosure to the tenant of the names and addresses of persons who:

1. Have power to negotiate, make repairs, etc., in the operation of the premises; and

2. Are empowered to receive service of notice and process that binds all of the owners.

In the absence of such disclosure the person collecting the rent shall be deemed to have the authority to accept notices and service and to provide for the necessary maintenance and repairs.

The purpose of this provisions is to enable the tenant to know to whom complaints must be made and, if repairs are not undertaken, the tenant the responsible parties who may be taken to court in order to enforce the provision.

Security Deposits

Due to difficulties in administering and accounting for security deposits, there have been some movement towards abolishing the security deposit. The URLTA preserves the security deposit, however, it limits the amount and prescribes certain penalties for its misuse. Under the

URLTA, a landlord is generally required to return the security deposit to the tenant within a specified time period after accounting for his claim to any part of the security deposit, e.g., for damages or non-payment of rent. The Act provides for a penalty in case the landlord fails to comply with this requirement.

Landlord's Obligations Upon Sale of Rental Property

The URLTA sets forth the obligations of the landlord after he or she sells the rental property. The Act relieves the landlord from liability under the lease for events occurring after a "good faith" sale to a bona fide purchaser, and after the tenant has been given written notice of the sale.

An exception exists concerning the tenant's security deposit and prepaid rent. Even after the sale has taken place, the original landlord is responsible for failure to account for the original tenant's security deposit and prepaid rent because the landlord should have taken steps to protect the tenant's funds at the time of the sale.

APPENDIX 1:
STATE TENANTS' RIGHTS LAWS

STATE	STATUTE
Alabama	Ala. Code §§ 35-9-1 to -100
Alaska	Alaska Stat. §§ 34.03.010 to .380
Arizona	Ariz. Rev. Stat. Ann. §§ 12-1171 to -1183; §§ 33-1301 to -1381
Arkansas	Ark. Code Ann. §§ 18-16-101 to -306
California	Cal. [Civ.] Code §§ 1925-1954, 1961-1962.7, 1995.010-1997.270
Colorado	Colo. Rev. Stat. §§ 38-12-101 to -104, -301 to -302
Connecticut	Conn. Gen. Stat. Ann. §§ 47a-1 to -51
Delaware	Del. Code. Ann. tit. 25, §§ 5101-7013
District of Columbia	D.C. Code Ann. §§ 42-3201 to -4097, -3501.01 to -3509.03
Florida	Fla. Stat. Ann. §§ 83.40-.66
Georgia	Ga. Code Ann. §§ 44-7-1 to -81
Hawaii	Haw. Rev. Stat. §§ 521-1 to -78
Idaho	Idaho Code §§ 6-301 to -324 and §§ 55-201 to -313
Illinois	Ill. Comp. Stat. ch. 765 para. 705/0.01-740/5
Indiana	Ind. Code Ann. §§ 32-7-1-1 to 37-7-9-10
Iowa	Iowa Code Ann. §§ 562A.1-.36
Kansas	Kan. Stat. Ann. §§ 58-2501 to -2573
Kentucky	Ky. Rev. Stat. Ann. §§ 383.010-.715
Louisiana	La. Rev. Stat. Ann. §§ 9:3201-:3259; La. Civ. Code Ann. art. 2669-2742
Maine	Me. Rev. Stat. Ann. tit. 14, §§ 6001-6046
Maryland	Md. Real Prop. Code Ann., §§ 8-101 to -604
Massachusetts	Mass. Gen. Laws Ann. ch. 186 §§ 1-21
Michigan	Mich. Comp. Laws Ann. § 554.601-.640
Minnesota	Minn. Stat. Ann. §§ 504B.001 to 504B.471

Mississippi	Miss. Code Ann. §§ 89-8-1 to -27
Missouri	Mo. Ann. Stat. §§ 441.005 to .880; and §§ 535.150-.300
Montana	Mont. Code Ann. §§ 70-24-101 to -25-206
Nebraska	Neb. Rev. Stat. §§ 76-1401 to -1449
Nevada	Nev. Rev. Stat. Ann. §§ 118A.010-.520
New Hampshire.	N.H. Rev. Stat. Ann. §§ 540:1 to 540:29; 540-A:1-540-A:8
New Jersey	N.J. Stat. Ann. §§ 46:8-1 to-49
New Mexico	N.M. Stat. Ann. §§ 47-8-1 to -51
New York	N.Y. Real Property Law ("RPL") §§ 220-238; Real Property Actions and Proceedings Law ("RPAPL")§§ 701-853; Multiple Dwelling Law ("MDL") all; Multiple Residence Law ("MRL") all; General Obligation Law ("GOL") §§ 7-103-108
North Carolina	N.C. Gen. Stat. §§ 42-1 to 42-14.2; 42-25-6 to 42-76
North Dakota	N.D. Cent. Code §§ 47-16-01 to -41
Ohio	Ohio Rev. Code Ann. §§ 5321.01-.19
Oklahoma	Okla. Stat. Ann. tit. 41, §§ 1-136
Oregon	Or. Rev. Stat. §§ 90.100-.450
Pennsylvania	Pa. Stat. Ann. tit. 68, §§ 250.101-.510-B
Rhode Island	R.I. Gen. Laws §§ 34-18-1 to -57
South Carolina	S.C. Code Ann. §§ 27-40-10 to -910
South Dakota	S.D. Codified Laws Ann. §§ 43-32-1 to -29
Tennessee	Tenn. Code Ann. §§ 66-28-101 to -520
Texas	Tex. Prop. Code Ann. §§ 91.001-92.354
Utah	Utah Code Ann. §§ 57-17-1 to -5, -22-1 to -6
Vermont	Vt. Stat Ann. tit. 9, §§ 4451-4468
Virginia	Va. Code Ann. §§ 55-218.1 to -248.40
Washington	Wash. Rev. Code Ann. §§ 59.04.010-.900, .18.010-.911
West Virginia	W. Va. Code §§ 37-6-1 to -30
Wisconsin	Wis. Stat. Ann. §§ 704.01-.45
Wyoming	Wyo. Stat. §§ 1-21-1201 to -1211; 34-2-128 to -129

APPENDIX 2:
SAMPLE CHARACTER REFERENCE LETTER

Date
Landlord Name
Street Address
City/State/Zip Code

Re: Ms. Mary Smith

To Whom It May Concern:

I am writing on behalf of Mary Smith, an applicant for your rental property located at [address of property]. I strongly recommend her as a tenant in your building. I have been a close personal friend of Mary Smith for over five years.

During this time, Mary Smith and I lived next door to each other in the same apartment building. I have had the opportunity to visit Mary's apartment on many occasions, and can assure you that she takes very good care of her residence. Her apartment is always clean and in good repair.

I can also assure you that Mary is a quiet and law-abiding tenant. She does not play loud music or entertain frequently. In addition, Mary is extremely diligent in paying her bills on time; therefore, you can be confident she will pay her rent promptly. I am certain you will be quite pleased to have Mary Smith as a tenant in your building.

If you have any questions or need further information, please feel free to contact me at [telephone number].

Sincerely,

Signature Line
Linda Jones
Street Address
City/State/Zip Code

APPENDIX 3:
SAMPLE RENTAL APPLICATION

RENTAL APPLICATION FOR

[INSERT RENTAL PROPERTY ADDRESS]

PREMISES TO BE LEASED

Address:

Description of Rental Property: Parking Facilities:

PROPOSED LEASE TERMS

Commencement Date of Lease: Lease Term:

Monthly Rent:

Security Deposit:

Application Fee:

Number of Occupants:

Do You Own Any Pets: [YES/NO]

APPLICANT INFORMATION

Applicant Name: Current Address:

Home Telephone Number:

Work Telephone Number:

Cell Phone Number:

Fax Number:

Driver's License Number:

Social Security Number:

EMPLOYMENT HISTORY

Present Occupation:

Employer Name and Address:

Employer Telephone Number:

Employer Contact Person:

Length of Time Employed:

Present Salary:

Previous Employer (if less than 5 years with present landlord):

Name/Address/Telephone Number:

FINANCIAL INFORMATION

Bank Name and Address:

Bank Telephone Number:

Contact Person:

Checking Account Number:

Savings Account Number:

REFERENCES

Credit References:

Name/Address/Telephone Number:

Name/Address/Telephone Number:

Name/Address/Telephone Number:

Personal References:

Name/Address/Telephone Number:

Name/Address/Telephone Number:

Name/Address/Telephone Number:

Present Landlord:

Name/Address/Telephone Number:

Previous Landlord (if less than 5 years with present landlord):

Name/Address/Telephone Number:

CONSENT TO CONTACT REFERENCES AND OBTAIN CREDIT REPORT

As part of my rental application, I hereby authorize and give my consent to [Name of Landlord] to contact all references named in this application, and to conduct a credit review, including obtaining my credit report and credit score from any authorized credit reporting agency.

I declare under penalty of perjury that the information listed in this application is true and correct.

DATED:

_____

APPLICANT NAME

APPENDIX 4:
DIRECTORY OF HUD FAIR HOUSING
REGIONAL OFFICES

REGION	ADDRESS	TELEPHONE	TTY
CONNECTICUT, MAINE, MASSACHUSETTS, NEW HAMPSHIRE. RHODE ISLAND, VERMONT	Boston Regional Office of FHEO U.S. Department of Housing and Urban Development (HUD) 10 Causeway Street Room 321 Boston, MA 02222-1092	617-994-8300/ 800-827-5005	617-565-5453
NEW JERSEY, NEW YORK	New York Regional Office of FHEO U.S. Department of Housing and Urban Development (HUD) 26 Federal Plaza Room 3532 New York, NY 10278-0068	212-542-7519/ 800-496-4294	212-264-0927
DELAWARE, DISTRICT OF COLUMBIA, MARYLAND, PENNSYLVANIA, VIRGINIA, WEST VIRGINIA	Philadelphia Regional Office of FHEO U.S. Department of Housing and Urban Development (HUD) The Wanamaker Building 100 Penn Square East 12TH Fl. Philadelphia, PA 19107-3380	215-656-0663/ 888-799-2085	215-656-3450

REGION	ADDRESS	TELEPHONE	TTY
ALABAMA, CARIBBEAN, FLORIDA, GEORGIA, KENTUCKY, MISSISSIPPI, NORTH CAROLINA, SOUTH CAROLINA, TENNESSEE	Atlanta Regional Office of FHEO. U.S. Department of Housing and Urban Development (HUD) Five Points Plaza 40 Marietta Street 16th Fl. Atlanta, GA 30303-2806	404-331-5140/ 800-440-8091	404-730-2654
ILLINOIS, INDIANA, MICHIGAN, MINNESOTA, OHIO, WISCONSIN	Chicago Regional Office of FHEO U.S. Department of Housing and Urban Development (HUD) Ralph H. Metcalfe Federal Building 77 West Jackson Boulevard Room 2101 Chicago, IL 60604-3507	312-353-7776/ 800-765-9372	312-353-7143
ARKANSAS, LOUISIANA, NEW MEXICO, OKLAHOMA, TEXAS	Fort Worth Regional Office of FHEO, U.S. Department of Housing and Urban Development (HUD) 801 Cherry Street 27th Fl. Forth Worth, TX 76113-2905	817-978-5900/ 800-669-9777	817-978-5595
IOWA, KANSAS, MISSOURI, NEBRASKA	Kansas City Regional Office of FHEO U.S. Department of Housing and Urban Development (HUD) Gateway Tower II 400 State Avenue Room 200 Kansas City, KS 66101-2406	913-551-6958/ 800-743-5323	913-551-6972
COLORADO, MONTANA, NORTH DAKOTA, SOUTH DAKOTA, UTAH, WYOMING	Denver Regional Office of FHEO U.S. Department of Housing and Urban Development (HUD), 1670 Broadway Denver, CO 80202-4801	303-672-5437/ 800-877-7353	303-672-5248

REGION	ADDRESS	TELEPHONE	TTY
ARIZONA, CALIFORNIA, HAWAII, NEVADA	San Francisco Regional Office of FHEO U.S. Department of Housing and Urban Development (HUD) 600 Harrison Street 3rd Floor San Francisco, CA 94107-1387	415-489-6524/ 800-347-3739	415-436-6594

APPENDIX 5:
THE *FAIR HOUSING ACT*

SEC. 3601. DECLARATION OF POLICY

It is the policy of the United States to provide, within constitutional limitations, for fair housing throughout the United States.

SEC. 3602. DEFINITIONS

As used in this subchapter—

(a) "Secretary" means the Secretary of Housing and Urban Development.

(b) "Dwelling" means any building, structure, or portion thereof which is occupied as, or designed or intended for occupancy as, a residence by one or more families, and any vacant land which is offered for sale or lease for the construction or location thereon of any such building, structure, or portion thereof.

(c) "Family" includes a single individual.

(d) "Person" includes one or more individuals, corporations, partnerships, associations, labor organizations, legal representatives, mutual companies, joint-stock companies, trusts, unincorporated organizations, trustees, trustees in cases under title 11 [of the United States Code], receivers, and fiduciaries.

(e) "To rent" includes to lease, to sublease, to let and otherwise to grant for a consideration the right to occupy premises not owned by the occupant.

(f) "Discriminatory housing practice" means an act that is unlawful under section 804, 805, 806, or 818 of this title.

(g) "State" means any of the several States, the District of Columbia, the Commonwealth of Puerto Rico, or any of the territories and possessions of the United States.

(h) "Handicap" means, with respect to a person—

(1) a physical or mental impairment which substantially limits one or more of such person's major life activities,

(2) a record of having such an impairment, or

(3) being regarded as having such an impairment, but such term does not include current, illegal use of or addiction to a controlled substance (as defined in section 802 of title 21).

(i) "Aggrieved person" includes any person who—

(1) claims to have been injured by a discriminatory housing practice; or

(2) believes that such person will be injured by a discriminatory housing practice that is about to occur.

(j) "Complainant" means the person (including the Secretary) who files a complaint under section 3610 of this title.

(k) "Familial status" means one or more individuals (who have not attained the age of 18 years) being domiciled with—

(1) a parent or another person having legal custody of such individual or individuals; or

(2) the designee of such parent or other person having such custody, with the written permission of such parent or other person.

The protections afforded against discrimination on the basis of familial status shall apply to any person who is pregnant or is in the process of securing legal custody of any individual who has not attained the age of 18 years.

(l) "Conciliation" means the attempted resolution of issues raised by a complaint, or by the investigation of such complaint, through informal negotiations involving the aggrieved person, the respondent, and the Secretary.

(m) "Conciliation agreement" means a written agreement setting forth the resolution of the issues in conciliation.

(n) "Respondent" means—

(1) the person or other entity accused in a complaint of an unfair housing practice; and

(2) any other person or entity identified in the course of investigation and notified as required with respect to respondents so identified under section 810(a).

(o) "Prevailing party" has the same meaning as such term has in section 1988 of this title.

SEC. 3603. EFFECTIVE DATES OF CERTAIN PROHIBITIONS

(a) Subject to the provisions of subsection (b) of this section and section 807 of this title, the prohibitions against discrimination in the sale or rental of housing set forth in section 3607 of this title, the prohibitions against discrimination in the sale or rental of housing set forth in section 3604 of this title shall apply:

(1) Upon enactment of this subchapter, to—

(A) dwellings owned or operated by the Federal Government;

(B) dwellings provided in whole or in part with the aid of loans, advances, grants, or contributions made by the Federal Government, under agreements entered into after November 20, 1962, unless payment due thereon has been made in full prior to April 11, 1968;

(C) dwellings provided in whole or in part by loans insured, guaranteed, or otherwise secured by the credit of the Federal Government, under agreements entered into after November 20, 1962, unless payment thereon has been made in full prior to April 11, 1968: Provided, That nothing contained in subparagraphs (B) and (C) of this subsection shall be applicable to dwellings solely by virtue of the fact that they are subject to mortgages held by an FDIC or FSLIC institution; and

(D) dwellings provided by the development or the redevelopment of real property purchased, rented, or otherwise obtained from a State or local public agency receiving Federal financial assistance for slum clearance or urban renewal with respect to such real property under loan or grant contracts entered into after November 20, 1962.

(2) After December 31, 1968, to all dwellings covered by paragraph (1) and to all other dwellings except as exempted by subsection (b) of this section.

(b) Nothing in section 3604 of this title (other than subsection (c)) shall apply to—

(1) any single-family house sold or rented by an owner: Provided, That such private individual owner does not own more than three such single-family houses at any one time: Provided further, That in the case of the sale of any such single-family house by a private individual owner not residing in such house at the time of such sale or

who was not the most recent resident of such house prior to such sale, the exemption granted by this subsection shall apply only with respect to one such sale within any twenty-four month period: Provided further, That such bona fide private individual owner does not own any interest in, nor is there owned or reserved on his behalf, under any express or voluntary agreement, title to or any right to all or a portion of the proceeds from the sale or rental of, more than three such single-family houses at any one time: Provided further, That after December 31, 1969, the sale or rental of any such single-family house shall be excepted from the application of this subchapter only if such house is sold or rented (A) without the use in any manner of the sales or rental facilities or the sales or rental services of any real estate broker, agent, or salesman, or of such facilities or services of any person in the business of selling or renting dwellings, or of any employee or agent of any such broker, agent, salesman, or person and (B) without the publication, posting or mailing, after notice, of any advertisement or written notice in violation of section 804(c) of this title; but nothing in this proviso shall prohibit the use of attorneys, escrow agents, abstractors, title companies, and other such professional assistance as necessary to perfect or transfer the title, or

(2) rooms or units in dwellings containing living quarters occupied or intended to be occupied by no more than four families living independently of each other, if the owner actually maintains and occupies one of such living quarters as his residence.

(c) or the purposes of subsection (b) of this section, a person shall be deemed to be in the business of selling or renting dwellings if—

(1) he has, within the preceding twelve months, participated as principal in three or more transactions involving the sale or rental of any dwelling or any interest therein, or

(2) he has, within the preceding twelve months, participated as agent, other than in the sale of his own personal residence in providing sales or rental facilities or sales or rental services in two or more transactions involving the sale or rental of any dwelling or any interest therein, or

(3) he is the owner of any dwelling designed or intended for occupancy by, or occupied by, five or more families.

SEC. 3604. DISCRIMINATION IN SALE OR RENTAL OF HOUSING AND OTHER PROHIBITED PRACTICES

As made applicable by section 3603 of this title and except as exempted by sections 3603(b) and 3607 of this title, it shall be unlawful—

(a) To refuse to sell or rent after the making of a bona fide offer, or to refuse to negotiate for the sale or rental of, or otherwise make unavailable or deny, a dwelling to any person because of race, color, religion, sex, familial status, or national origin.

(b) To discriminate against any person in the terms, conditions, or privileges of sale or rental of a dwelling, or in the provision of services or facilities in connection therewith, because of race, color, religion, sex, familial status, or national origin.

(c) To make, print, or publish, or cause to be made, printed, or published any notice, statement, or advertisement, with respect to the sale or rental of a dwelling that indicates any preference, limitation, or discrimination based on race, color, religion, sex, handicap, familial status, or national origin, or an intention to make any such preference, limitation, or discrimination.

(d) To represent to any person because of race, color, religion, sex, handicap, familial status, or national origin that any dwelling is not available for inspection, sale, or rental when such dwelling is in fact so available.

(e) For profit, to induce or attempt to induce any person to sell or rent any dwelling by representations regarding the entry or prospective entry into the neighborhood of a person or persons of a particular race, color, religion, sex, handicap, familial status, or national origin.

(f) (1) To discriminate in the sale or rental, or to otherwise make unavailable or deny, a dwelling to any buyer or renter because of a handicap of—

(A) that buyer or renter,

(B) a person residing in or intending to reside in that dwelling after it is so sold, rented, or made available; or

(C) any person associated with that buyer or renter.

(2) To discriminate against any person in the terms, conditions, or privileges of sale or rental of a dwelling, or in the provision of services or facilities in connection with such dwelling, because of a handicap of—

(A) that person; or

(B) a person residing in or intending to reside in that dwelling after it is so sold, rented, or made available; or

(C) any person associated with that person.

(3) For purposes of this subsection, discrimination includes—

(A) a refusal to permit, at the expense of the handicapped person, reasonable modifications of existing premises occupied or to be occupied by such person if such modifications may be necessary to afford such person full enjoyment of the premises, except that, in the case of a rental, the landlord may where it is reasonable to do so condition permission for a modification on the renter agreeing to restore the interior of the premises to the condition that existed before the modification, reasonable wear and tear excepted.

(B) a refusal to make reasonable accommodations in rules, policies, practices, or services, when such accommodations may be necessary to afford such person equal opportunity to use and enjoy a dwelling; or

(C) in connection with the design and construction of covered multifamily dwellings for first occupancy after the date that is 30 months after the date of enactment of the Fair Housing Amendments Act of 1988, a failure to design and construct those dwelling in such a manner that—

(i) the public use and common use portions of such dwellings are readily accessible to and usable by handicapped persons;

(ii) all the doors designed to allow passage into and within all premises within such dwellings are sufficiently wide to allow passage by handicapped persons in wheelchairs; and

(iii) all premises within such dwellings contain the following features of adaptive design:

(I) an accessible route into and through the dwelling;

(II) light switches, electrical outlets, thermostats, and other environmental controls in accessible locations;

(III) reinforcements in bathroom walls to allow later installation of grab bars; and

(IV) usable kitchens and bathrooms such that an individual in a wheelchair can maneuver about the space.

(4) Compliance with the appropriate requirements of the American National Standard for buildings and facilities providing accessibility and usability for physically handicapped people (commonly cited as

"ANSI A117.1") suffices to satisfy the requirements of paragraph (3)(C)(iii).

(5)(A) If a State or unit of general local government has incorporated into its laws the requirements set forth in paragraph (3)(C), compliance with such laws shall be deemed to satisfy the requirements of that paragraph.

(B) A State or unit of general local government may review and approve newly constructed covered multifamily dwellings for the purpose of making determinations as to whether the design and construction requirements of paragraph (3)(C) are met.

(C) The Secretary shall encourage, but may not require, States and units of local government to include in their existing procedures for the review and approval of newly constructed covered multifamily dwellings, determinations as to whether the design and construction of such dwellings are consistent with paragraph (3)(C), and shall provide technical assistance to States and units of local government and other persons to implement the requirements of paragraph (3)(C).

(D) Nothing in this title shall be construed to require the Secretary to review or approve the plans, designs or construction of all covered multifamily dwellings, to determine whether the design and construction of such dwellings are consistent with the requirements of paragraph 3(C).

(6)(A) Nothing in paragraph (5) shall be construed to affect the authority and responsibility of the Secretary or a State or local public agency certified pursuant to section 810(f)(3) of this Act to receive and process complaints or otherwise engage in enforcement activities under this title.

(B) Determinations by a State or a unit of general local government under paragraphs (5)(A) and (B) shall not be conclusive in enforcement proceedings under this title.

(7) As used in this subsection, the term "covered multifamily dwellings" means—

(A) buildings consisting of 4 or more units if such buildings have one or more elevators; and

(B) ground floor units in other buildings consisting of 4 or more units.

(8) Nothing in this title shall be construed to invalidate or limit any law of a State or political subdivision of a State, or other jurisdiction in which this title shall be effective, that requires dwellings to be de-

signed and constructed in a manner that affords handicapped persons greater access than is required by this title.

(9) Nothing in this subsection requires that a dwelling be made available to an individual whose tenancy would constitute a direct threat to the health or safety of other individuals or whose tenancy would result in substantial physical damage to the property of others.

SEC. 3605. DISCRIMINATION IN RESIDENTIAL REAL ESTATE-RELATED TRANSACTIONS

(a) In General.—

It shall be unlawful for any person or other entity whose business includes engaging in residential real estate-related transactions to discriminate against any person in making available such a transaction, or in the terms or conditions of such a transaction, because of race, color, religion, sex, handicap, familial status, or national origin.

(b) Residential real estate-related transaction" defined

As used in this section, the term "residential real estate-related transaction" means any of the following:

(1) The making or purchasing of loans or providing other financial assistance—

(A) for purchasing, constructing, improving, repairing, or maintaining a dwelling; or

(B) secured by residential real estate.

(2) The selling, brokering, or appraising of residential real property.

(c) Appraisal Exemption.—Nothing in this title prohibits a person engaged in the business of furnishing appraisals of real property to take into consideration factors other than race, color, religion, national origin, sex, handicap, or familial status.

SEC. 3606. DISCRIMINATION IN PROVISION OF BROKERAGE SERVICES

After December 31, 1968, it shall be unlawful to deny any person access to or membership or participation in any multiple-listing service, real estate brokers' organization or other service, organization, or facility relating to the business of selling or renting dwellings, or to discriminate against him in the terms or conditions of such access, membership, or participation, on account of race, color, religion, sex, handicap, familial status, or national origin.

SEC. 3607. RELIGIOUS ORGANIZATION OR PRIVATE CLUB EXEMPTION

(a) Nothing in this subchapter shall prohibit a religious organization, association, or society, or any nonprofit institution or organization operated, supervised or controlled by or in conjunction with a religious organization, association, or society, from limiting the sale, rental or occupancy of dwellings which it owns or operates for other than a commercial purpose to persons of the same religion, or from giving preference to such persons, unless membership in such religion is restricted on account of race, color, or national origin. Nor shall anything in this subchapter prohibit a private club not in fact open to the public, which as an incident to its primary purpose or purposes provides lodgings which it owns or operates for other than a commercial purpose, from limiting the rental or occupancy of such lodgings to its members or from giving preference to its members.

(b)(1) Nothing in this title limits the applicability of any reasonable local, State, or Federal restrictions regarding the maximum number of occupants permitted to occupy a dwelling. Nor does any provision in this title regarding familial status apply with respect to housing for older persons.

(2) As used in this section "housing for older persons" means housing—

(A) provided under any State or Federal program that the Secretary determines is specifically designed and operated to assist elderly persons (as defined in the State or Federal program); or

(B) intended for, and solely occupied by, persons 62 years of age or older; or

(C) intended and operated for occupancy by persons 55 years of age or older, and—

(i) at least 80 percent of the occupied units are occupied by at least one person who is 55 years of age or older;

(ii) the housing facility or community publishes and adheres to policies and procedures that demonstrate the intent required under this subparagraph; and

(iii) the housing facility or community complies with rules issued by the Secretary for verification of occupancy, which shall—

(I) provide for verification by reliable surveys and affidavits; and

(II) include examples of the types of policies and procedures relevant to a determination of compliance with the requirement of clause (ii). Such surveys and affidavits shall be admissible in administrative and judicial proceedings for the purposes of such verification.

(3) Housing shall not fail to meet the requirements for housing for older persons by reason of:

(A) persons residing in such housing as of the date of enactment of this Act who do not meet the age requirements of subsections (2)(B) or (C): Provided, That new occupants of such housing meet the age requirements of sections (2)(B) or (C); or

(B) unoccupied units: Provided, That such units are reserved for occupancy by persons who meet the age requirements of subsections (2)(B) or (C).

(4) Nothing in this title prohibits conduct against a person because such person has been convicted by any court of competent jurisdiction of the illegal manufacture or distribution of a controlled substance as defined in section 802 of title 21.

(5)(A) A person shall not be held personally liable for monetary damages for a violation of this title if such person reasonably relied, in good faith, on the application of the exemption under this subsection relating to housing for older persons.

(B) For the purposes of this paragraph, a person may only show good faith reliance on the application of the exemption by showing that—

(i) such person has no actual knowledge that the facility or community is not, or will not be, eligible for such exemption; and

(ii) the facility or community has stated formally, in writing, that the facility or community complies with the requirements for such exemption.

SEC. 3608. ADMINISTRATION

(a) Authority and responsibility

The authority and responsibility for administering this Act shall be in the Secretary of Housing and Urban Development.

(b) Assistant Secretary

The Department of Housing and Urban Development shall be provided an additional Assistant Secretary.

(c) Delegation of authority; appointment of administrative law judges; location of conciliation meetings; administrative review

The Secretary may delegate any of his functions, duties and power to employees of the Department of Housing and Urban Development or to boards of such employees, including functions, duties, and powers with respect to investigating, conciliating, hearing, determining, ordering, certifying, reporting, or otherwise acting as to any work, business, or matter under this subchapter. The person to whom such delegations are made with respect to hearing functions, duties, and powers shall be appointed and shall serve in the Department of Housing and Urban Development in compliance with sections 3105, 3344, 5372, and 7521 of title 5 [of the United States Code]. Insofar as possible, conciliation meetings shall be held in the cities or other localities where the discriminatory housing practices allegedly occurred. The Secretary shall by rule prescribe such rights of appeal from the decisions of his administrative law judges to other administrative law judges or to other officers in the Department, to boards of officers or to himself, as shall be appropriate and in accordance with law.

(d) Cooperation of Secretary and executive departments and agencies in administration of housing and urban development programs and activities to further fair housing purposes

All executive departments and agencies shall administer their programs and activities relating to housing and urban development (including any Federal agency having regulatory or supervisory authority over financial institutions) in a manner affirmatively to further the purposes of this subchapter and shall cooperate with the Secretary to further such purposes.

(e) Functions of Secretary

The Secretary of Housing and Urban Development shall—

(1) make studies with respect to the nature and extent of discriminatory housing practices in representative communities, urban, suburban, and rural, throughout the United States;

(2) publish and disseminate reports, recommendations, and information derived from such studies, including an annual report to the Congress—

(A) specifying the nature and extent of progress made nationally in eliminating discriminatory housing practices and furthering the purposes of this title, obstacles remaining to achieving equal housing opportunity, and recommendations for further legislative or executive action; and

(B) containing tabulations of the number of instances (and the reasons therefor) in the preceding year in which—

(i) investigations are not completed as required by section 3610(a)(1)(B);

(ii) determinations are not made within the time specified in section 3610(g); and

(iii) hearings are not commenced or findings and conclusions are not made as required by section 812(g);

(3) cooperate with and render technical assistance to Federal, State, local, and other public or private agencies, organizations, and institutions which are formulating or carrying on programs to prevent or eliminate discriminatory housing practices;

(4) cooperate with and render such technical and other assistance to the Community Relations Service as may be appropriate to further its activities in preventing or eliminating discriminatory housing practices;

(5) administer the programs and activities relating to housing and urban development in a manner affirmatively to further the policies of this subchapter; and

(6) annually report to the Congress, and make available to the public, data on the race, color, religion, sex, national origin, age, handicap, and family characteristics of persons and households who are applicants for, participants in, or beneficiaries or potential beneficiaries of, programs administered by the Department to the extent such characteristics are within the coverage of the provisions of law and Executive orders referred to in subsection (f) which apply to such programs (and in order to develop the data to be included and made available to the public under this subsection, the Secretary shall, without regard to any other provision of law, collect such information relating to those characteristics as the Secretary determines to be necessary or appropriate).

(f) The provisions of law and Executive orders to which subsection (e)(6) applies are—

(1) title VI of the Civil Rights Act of 1964 [42 U.S.C. 2000d et seq.];

(2) this subchapter;

(3) section 794 of title 29;

(4) the Age Discrimination Act of 1975 [42 U.S.C. 6101 et seq.];

(5) the Equal Credit Opportunity Act [15 U.S.C. 1691 et seq.];

(6) section 1982 of this title;

(7) section 637(a) of title 15;

(8) section 1735f-5 of title 12;

(9) section 5309 of this title;

(10) section 1701u of title 12;

(11) Executive orders 11063, 11246, 11625, 12250, 12259, and 12432; and

(12) any other provision of law which the Secretary specifies by publication in the Federal Register for the purpose of this subsection.

SEC. 3608A. COLLECTION OF CERTAIN DATA

(a) In general

To assess the extent of compliance with Federal fair housing requirements (including the requirements established under title VI of Public Law 88-352 [42 U.S.C. 2000d et seq.] and title VIII of Public Law 90-284 [42 U.S.C. 3601 et seq.]), the Secretary of Agriculture shall collect, not less than annually, data on the racial and ethnic characteristics of persons eligible for, assisted, or otherwise benefiting under each community development, housing assistance, and mortgage and loan insurance and guarantee program administered by such Secretary. Such data shall be collected on a building by building basis if the Secretary determines such collection to be appropriate.

(b) Reports to Congress

The Secretary of Housing and Urban Development and the Secretary of Agriculture shall each include in the annual report of such Secretary to the Congress a summary and evaluation of the data collected by such Secretary under subsection (a) of this section during the preceding year.

SEC. 3609. EDUCATION AND CONCILIATION; CONFERENCES AND CONSULTATIONS; REPORTS

Immediately after April 11, 1968, the Secretary shall commence such educational and conciliatory activities as in his judgment will further the purposes of this subchapter. He shall call conferences of persons in the housing industry and other interested parties to acquaint them with the provisions of this subchapter and his suggested means of implementing it, and shall endeavor with their advice to work out programs of voluntary compliance and of enforcement. He may pay per diem, travel, and transportation expenses for persons attending such conferences as provided in section 5703 of Title 5. He shall consult with State and local officials and other interested parties to learn the extent, if any, to which housing discrimination exists in their State or locality, and whether and how State or local enforcement programs might be utilized to combat such discrimination in connection with or in place of, the Secretary's enforcement of this subchapter. The Secretary shall issue reports on such conferences and consultations as he deems appropriate.

SEC. 3610. ADMINISTRATIVE ENFORCEMENT; PRELIMINARY MATTERS

(a) Complaints and Answers.—

(1) (A) (i) An aggrieved person may, not later than one year after an alleged discriminatory housing practice has occurred or terminated, file a complaint with the Secretary alleging such discriminatory housing practice. The Secretary, on the Secretary's own initiative, may also file such a complaint.

(ii) Such complaints shall be in writing and shall contain such information and be in such form as the Secretary requires.

(iii) The Secretary may also investigate housing practices to determine whether a complaint should be brought under this section.

(B) Upon the filing of such a complaint—

(i) the Secretary shall serve notice upon the aggrieved person acknowledging such filing and advising the aggrieved person of the time limits and choice of forums provided under this title;

(ii) the Secretary shall, not later than 10 days after such filing or the identification of an additional respondent under paragraph (2), serve on the respondent a notice identifying the alleged discriminatory housing practice and advising such respondent of the procedural rights and obligations of respondents under this title, together with a copy of the original complaint;

(iii) each respondent may file, not later than 10 days after receipt of notice from the Secretary, an answer to such complaint; and

(iv) the Secretary shall make an investigation of the alleged discriminatory housing practice and complete such investigation within 100 days after the filing of the complaint (or, when the Secretary takes further action under subsection (f)(2) with respect to a complaint, within 100 days after the commencement of such further action), unless it is impracticable to do so.

(C) If the Secretary is unable to complete the investigation within 100 days after the filing of the complaint (or, when the Secretary takes further action under subsection (f)(2) with respect to a complaint, within 100 days after the commencement of such further action), the Secretary shall notify the complainant and respondent in writing of the reasons for not doing so.

(D) Complaints and answers shall be under oath or affirmation, and may be reasonably and fairly amended at any time.

(2)(A) A person who is not named as a respondent in a complaint, but who is identified as a respondent in the course of investigation, may be joined as an additional or substitute respondent upon written notice, under paragraph (1), to such person, from the Secretary.

(B) Such notice, in addition to meeting the requirements of paragraph (1), shall explain the basis for the Secretary's belief that the person to whom the notice is addressed is properly joined as a respondent.

(b) Investigative Report and Conciliation.—

(1) During the period beginning with the filing of such complaint and ending with the filing of a charge or a dismissal by the Secretary, the Secretary shall, to the extent feasible, engage in conciliation with respect to such complaint.

(2) A conciliation agreement arising out of such conciliation shall be an agreement between the respondent and the complainant, and shall be subject to approval by the Secretary.

(3) A conciliation agreement may provide for binding arbitration of the dispute arising from the complaint. Any such arbitration that results from a conciliation agreement may award appropriate relief, including monetary relief.

(4) Each conciliation agreement shall be made public unless the complainant and respondent otherwise agree and the Secretary determines that disclosure is not required to further the purposes of this title.

(5)(A) At the end of each investigation under this section, the Secretary shall prepare a final investigative report containing—

(i) the names and dates of contacts with witnesses;

(ii) a summary and the dates of correspondence and other contacts with the aggrieved person and the respondent;

(iii) a summary description of other pertinent records;

(iv) a summary of witness statements; and

(v) answers to interrogatories.

(B) A final report under this paragraph may be amended if additional evidence is later discovered.

(c) Failure to Comply With Conciliation Agreement.—

Whenever the Secretary has reasonable cause to believe that a respondent has breached a conciliation agreement, the Secretary shall refer the matter to the Attorney General with a recommendation that a civil action be filed under section 3614 for the enforcement of such agreement.

(d) Prohibitions and Requirements With Respect to Disclosure of Information.—

(1) Nothing said or done in the course of conciliation under this title may be made public or used as evidence in a subsequent proceeding under this title without the written consent of the persons concerned.

(2) Notwithstanding paragraph (1), the Secretary shall make available to the aggrieved person and the respondent, at any time, upon request following completion of the Secretary's investigation, information derived from an investigation and any final investigative report relating to that investigation.

(e) Prompt Judicial Action.—

(1) If the Secretary concludes at any time following the filing of a complaint that prompt judicial action is necessary to carry out the purposes of this title, the Secretary may authorize a civil action for appropriate temporary or preliminary relief pending final disposition of the complaint under this section. Upon receipt of such authorization, the Attorney General shall promptly commence and maintain such an action. Any temporary restraining order or other order granting preliminary or temporary relief shall be issued in accordance with the Federal Rules of Civil Procedure. The commencement of a civil action under this subsection does not affect the initiation or continuation of administrative proceedings under this section and section 3612 of this title.

(2) Whenever the Secretary has reason to believe that a basis may exist for the commencement of proceedings against any respondent under section 3614(a) and 3614(c) or for proceedings by any governmental licensing or supervisory authorities, the Secretary shall transmit the information upon which such belief is based to the Attorney General, or to such authorities, as the case may be.

(f) Referral for State or Local Proceedings.—

(1) Whenever a complaint alleges a discriminatory housing practice—

(A) within the jurisdiction of a State or local public agency; and

(B) as to which such agency has been certified by the Secretary under this subsection; the Secretary shall refer such complaint to that certified agency before taking any action with respect to such complaint.

(2) Except with the consent of such certified agency, the Secretary, after that referral is made, shall take no further action with respect to such complaint unless—

(A) the certified agency has failed to commence proceedings with respect to the complaint before the end of the 30th day after the date of such referral;

(B) the certified agency, having so commenced such proceedings, fails to carry forward such proceedings with reasonable promptness; or

(C) the Secretary determines that the certified agency no longer qualifies for certification under this subsection with respect to the relevant jurisdiction.

(3)(A) The Secretary may certify an agency under this subsection only if the Secretary determines that—

(i) the substantive rights protected by such agency in the jurisdiction with respect to which certification is to be made;

(ii) the procedures followed by such agency;

(iii) the remedies available to such agency; and

(iv) the availability of judicial review of such agency's action; are substantially equivalent to those created by and under this title.

(B) Before making such certification, the Secretary shall take into account the current practices and past performance, if any, of such agency.

(4) During the period which begins on the date of the enactment of the Fair Housing Amendments Act of 1988 and ends 40 months after such date, each agency certified (including an agency certified for interim referrals pursuant to 24 CFR 115.11, unless such agency is subsequently denied recognition under 24 CFR 115.7) for the purposes of this title on the day before such date shall for the purposes of this subsection be considered certified under this subsection with respect to those matters for which such agency was certified on that date. If the Secretary determines in an individual case that an agency has not been

able to meet the certification requirements within this 40-month period due to exceptional circumstances, such as the infrequency of legislative sessions in that jurisdiction, the Secretary may extend such period by not more than 8 months.

(5) Not less frequently than every 5 years, the Secretary shall determine whether each agency certified under this subsection continues to qualify for certification. The Secretary shall take appropriate action with respect to any agency not so qualifying.

(g) Reasonable Cause Determination and Effect.—

(1) The Secretary shall, within 100 days after the filing of the complaint (or, when the Secretary takes further action under subsection (f)(2) with respect to a complaint, within 100 days after the commencement of such further action), determine based on the facts whether reasonable cause exists to believe that a discriminatory housing practice has occurred or is about to occur, unless it is impracticable to do so, or unless the Secretary has approved a conciliation agreement with respect to the complaint. If the Secretary is unable to make the determination within 100 days after the filing of the complaint (or, when the Secretary takes further action under subsection (f)(2) with respect to a complaint, within 100 days after the commencement of such further action), the Secretary shall notify the complainant and respondent in writing of the reasons for not doing so.

(2)(A) If the Secretary determines that reasonable cause exists to believe that a discriminatory housing practice has occurred or is about to occur, the Secretary shall, except as provided in subparagraph (C), immediately issue a charge on behalf of the aggrieved person, for further proceedings under section 812.

(B) Such charge—

(i) shall consist of a short and plain statement of the facts upon which the Secretary has found reasonable cause to believe that a discriminatory housing practice has occurred or is about to occur;

(ii) shall be based on the final investigative report; and

(iii) need not be limited to the facts or grounds alleged in the complaint filed under section 810(a).

(C) If the Secretary determines that the matter involves the legality of any State or local zoning or other land use law or ordinance, the Secretary shall immediately refer the matter to the Attorney General for appropriate action under section 814, instead of issuing such charge.

(3) If the Secretary determines that no reasonable cause exists to believe that a discriminatory housing practice has occurred or is about to occur, the Secretary shall promptly dismiss the complaint. The Secretary shall make public disclosure of each such dismissal.

(4) The Secretary may not issue a charge under this section regarding an alleged discriminatory housing practice after the beginning of the trial of a civil action commenced by the aggrieved party under an Act of Congress or a State law, seeking relief with respect to that discriminatory housing practice.

(h) Service of Copies of Charge.—

After the Secretary issues a charge under this section, the Secretary shall cause a copy thereof, together with information as to how to make an election under section 812(a) and the effect of such an election, to be served—

(1) on each respondent named in such charge, together with a notice of opportunity for a hearing at a time and place specified in the notice, unless that election is made; and

(2) on each aggrieved person on whose behalf the complaint was filed.

SEC. 3611. SUBPOENAS; GIVING OF EVIDENCE

(a) In General.—

The Secretary may, in accordance with this subsection, issue subpoenas and order discovery in aid of investigations and hearings under this title. Such subpoenas and discovery may be ordered to the same extent and subject to the same limitations as would apply if the subpoenas or discovery were ordered or served in aid of a civil action in the United States district court for the district in which the investigation is taking place.

(b) Witness Fees.—

Witnesses summoned by a subpoena under this title shall be entitled to same witness and mileage fees as witnesses in proceedings in United States district courts. Fees payable to a witness summoned by a subpoena issued at the request of a party shall be paid by that party or, where a party is unable to pay the fees, by the Secretary.

(c) Criminal Penalties.—

(1) Any person who willfully fails or neglects to attend and testify or to answer any lawful inquiry or to produce records, documents, or other evidence, if it is in such person's power to do so, in obedience to the

subpoena or other lawful order under subsection (a), shall be fined not more than $100,000 or imprisoned not more than one year, or both.

(2) Any person who, with intent thereby to mislead another person in any proceeding under this title—

(A) makes or causes to be made any false entry or statement of fact in any report, account, record, or other document produced pursuant to subpoena or other lawful order under subsection (a);

(B) willfully neglects or fails to make or to cause to be made full, true, and correct entries in such reports, accounts, records, or other documents; or

(C) willfully mutilates, alters, or by any other means falsifies any documentary evidence;

shall be fined not more than $100,000 or imprisoned not more than one year, or both.

SEC. 3612. ENFORCEMENT BY SECRETARY

(a) Election of Judicial Determination.—

When a charge is filed under section 3610, a complainant, a respondent, or an aggrieved person on whose behalf the complaint was filed, may elect to have the claims asserted in that charge decided in a civil action under subsection (o) in lieu of a hearing under subsection (b). The election must be made not later than 20 days after the receipt by the electing person of service under section 3610(h) or, in the case of the Secretary, not later than 20 days after such service. The person making such election shall give notice of doing so to the Secretary and to all other complainants and respondents to whom the charge relates.

(b) Administrative Law Judge Hearing in Absence of Election.—

If an election is not made under subsection (a) with respect to a charge filed under section 810, the Secretary shall provide an opportunity for a hearing on the record with respect to a charge issued under section 810. The Secretary shall delegate the conduct of a hearing under this section to an administrative law judge appointed under section 3105 of title 5, United States Code. The administrative law judge shall conduct the hearing at a place in the vicinity in which the discriminatory housing practice is alleged to have occurred or to be about to occur.

(c) Rights of Parties.—

At a hearing under this section, each party may appear in person, be represented by counsel, present evidence, cross-examine witnesses, and obtain the issuance of subpoenas under section 3611. Any aggrieved person may intervene as a party in the proceeding. The Federal Rules of Evidence apply to the presentation of evidence in such hearing as they would in a civil action in a United States district court.

(d) Expedited Discovery and Hearing.—

(1) Discovery in administrative proceedings under this section shall be conducted as expeditiously and inexpensively as possible, consistent with the need of all parties to obtain relevant evidence.

(2) A hearing under this section shall be conducted as expeditiously and inexpensively as possible, consistent with the needs and rights of the parties to obtain a fair hearing and a complete record.

(3) The Secretary shall, not later than 180 days after the date of enactment of this subsection, issue rules to implement this subsection.

(e) Resolution of Charge.—

Any resolution of a charge before a final order under this section shall require the consent of the aggrieved person on whose behalf the charge is issued.

(f) Effect of Trial of Civil Action on Administrative Proceedings.—

An administrative law judge may not continue administrative proceedings under this section regarding any alleged discriminatory housing practice after the beginning of the trial of a civil action commenced by the aggrieved party under an Act of Congress or a State law, seeking relief with respect to that discriminatory housing practice.

(g) Hearings, Findings and Conclusions, and Order.—

(1) The administrative law judge shall commence the hearing under this section no later than 120 days following the issuance of the charge, unless it is impracticable to do so. If the administrative law judge is unable to commence the hearing within 120 days after the issuance of the charge, the administrative law judge shall notify the Secretary, the aggrieved person on whose behalf the charge was filed, and the respondent, in writing of the reasons for not doing so.

(2) The administrative law judge shall make findings of fact and conclusions of law within 60 days after the end of the hearing under this section, unless it is impracticable to do so. If the administrative law judge is unable to make findings of fact and conclusions of law within such period, or any succeeding 60-day period thereafter, the administrative law judge shall notify the Secretary, the aggrieved person on whose behalf the charge was filed, and the respondent, in writing of the reasons for not doing so.

(3) If the administrative law judge finds that a respondent has engaged or is about to engage in a discriminatory housing practice, such administrative law judge shall promptly issue an order for such relief as may be appropriate, which may include actual damages suffered by the aggrieved person and injunctive or other equitable relief. Such order may, to vindicate the public interest, assess a civil penalty against the respondent—

(A) in an amount not exceeding $10,000 if the respondent has not been adjudged to have committed any prior discriminatory housing practice;

(B) in an amount not exceeding $25,000 if the respondent has been adjudged to have committed one other discriminatory housing practice during the 5-year period ending on the date of the filing of this charge; and

(C) in an amount not exceeding $50,000 if the respondent has been adjudged to have committed 2 or more discriminatory housing practices during the 7-year period ending on the date of the filing of this charge;

except that if the acts constituting the discriminatory housing practice that is the object of the charge are committed by the same natural person who has been previously adjudged to have committed acts constituting a discriminatory housing practice, then the civil penalties set forth in subparagraphs (B) and (C) may be imposed without regard to the period of time within which any subsequent discriminatory housing practice occurred.

(4) No such order shall affect any contract, sale, encumbrance, or lease consummated before the issuance of such order and involving a bona fide purchaser, encumbrancer, or tenant without actual notice of the charge filed under this title.

(5) In the case of an order with respect to a discriminatory housing practice that occurred in the course of a business subject to a licensing or regulation by a governmental agency, the Secretary shall, not later than 30 days after the date of the issuance of such order (or, if such order is judicially reviewed, 30 days after such order is in substance affirmed upon such review)—

(A) send copies of the findings of fact, conclusions of law, and the order, to that governmental agency; and

(B) recommend to that governmental agency appropriate disciplinary action (including, where appropriate, the suspension or revocation of the license of the respondent).

(6) In the case of an order against a respondent against whom another order was issued within the preceding 5 years under this section, the Secretary shall send a copy of each such order to the Attorney General.

(7) If the administrative law judge finds that the respondent has not engaged or is not about to engage in a discriminatory housing practice, as the case may be, such administrative law judge shall enter an order dismissing the charge. The Secretary shall make public disclosure of each such dismissal.

(h) Review by Secretary; Service of Final Order.—

(1) The Secretary may review any finding, conclusion, or order issued under subsection (g). Such review shall be completed not later than 30 days after the finding, conclusion, or order is so issued; otherwise the finding, conclusion, or order becomes final.

(2) The Secretary shall cause the findings of fact and conclusions of law made with respect to any final order for relief under this section, together with a copy of such order, to be served on each aggrieved person and each respondent in the proceeding.

(i) Judicial Review.—

(1) Any party aggrieved by a final order for relief under this section granting or denying in whole or in part the relief sought may obtain a review of such order under chapter 158 of title 28.

(2) Notwithstanding such chapter, venue of the proceeding shall be in the judicial circuit in which the discriminatory housing practice is alleged to have occurred, and filing of the petition for review shall be not later than 30 days after the order is entered.

(j) Court Enforcement of Administrative Order Upon Petition by Secretary.—

(1) The Secretary may petition any United States court of appeals for the circuit in which the discriminatory housing practice is alleged to have occurred or in which any respondent resides or transacts business for the enforcement of the order of the administrative law judge and for appropriate temporary relief or restraining order, by filing in such court a written petition praying that such order be enforced and for appropriate temporary relief or restraining order.

(2) The Secretary shall file in court with the petition the record in the proceeding. A copy of such petition shall be forthwith transmitted by the clerk of the court to the parties to the proceeding before the administrative law judge.

(k) Relief Which May Be Granted.—

(1) Upon the filing of a petition under subsection (i) or (j), the court may—

(A) grant to the petitioner, or any other party, such temporary relief, restraining order, or other order as the court deems just and proper;

(B) affirm, modify, or set aside, in whole or in part, the order, or remand the order for further proceedings; and

(C) enforce such order to the extent that such order is affirmed or modified.

(2) Any party to the proceeding before the administrative law judge may intervene in the court of appeals.

(3) No objection not made before the administrative law judge shall be considered by the court, unless the failure or neglect to urge such objection is excused because of extraordinary circumstances.

(l) Enforcement Decree in Absence of Petition for Review.—

If no petition for review is filed under subsection (i) before the expiration of 45 days after the date the administrative law judge's order is entered, the administrative law judge's findings of fact and order shall be conclusive in connection with any petition for enforcement—

(1) which is filed by the Secretary under subsection (j) after the end of such day; or

(2) under subsection (m) of this section.

(m) Court Enforcement of Administrative Order Upon Petition of Any Person Entitled to Relief.—

If before the expiration of 60 days after the date the administrative law judge's order is entered, no petition for review has been filed under subsection (i), and the Secretary has not sought enforcement of the order under subsection (j), any person entitled to relief under the order may petition for a decree enforcing the order in the United States court of appeals for the circuit in which the discriminatory housing practice is alleged to have occurred.

(n) Entry of Decree.—

The clerk of the court of appeals in which a petition for enforcement is filed under subsection (1) or (m) shall forthwith enter a decree enforcing the order and shall transmit a copy of such decree to the Secretary, the respondent named in the petition, and to any other parties to the proceeding before the administrative law judge.

(o) Civil Action for Enforcement When Election Is Made for Such Civil Action.—

(1) If an election is made under subsection (a), the Secretary shall authorize, and not later than 30 days after the election is made the Attorney General shall commence and maintain, a civil action on behalf of the aggrieved person in a United States district court seeking relief under this subsection. Venue for such civil action shall be determined under chapter 87 of title 28, United States Code.

(2) Any aggrieved person with respect to the issues to be determined in a civil action under this subsection may intervene as of right in that civil action.

(3) In a civil action under this subsection, if the court finds that a discriminatory housing practice has occurred or is about to occur, the court may grant as relief any relief which a court could grant with respect to such discriminatory housing practice in a civil action under section 3613. Any relief so granted that would accrue to an aggrieved person in a civil action commenced by that aggrieved person under section 3613 shall also accrue to that aggrieved person in a civil action under this subsection. If monetary relief is sought for the benefit of an aggrieved person who does not intervene in the civil action, the court shall not award such relief if that aggrieved person has not complied with discovery orders entered by the court.

(p) Attorney's Fees.—

In any administrative proceeding brought under this section, or any court proceeding arising therefrom, or any civil action under this section, the administrative law judge or the court, as the case may be, in its discretion, may allow the prevailing party, other than the United States, a reasonable attorney's fee and costs. The United States shall be liable for such fees and costs to the extent provided by section 504 of title 5, United States Code, or by section 2412 of title 28, United States Code.

SEC. 3613. ENFORCEMENT BY PRIVATE PERSONS

(a) Civil Action.—

(1)(A) An aggrieved person may commence a civil action in an appropriate United States district court or State court not later than 2 years after the occurrence or the termination of an alleged discriminatory housing practice, or the breach of a conciliation agreement entered into under this title, whichever occurs last, to obtain appropriate relief with respect to such discriminatory housing practice or breach.

(B) The computation of such 2-year period shall not include any time during which an administrative proceeding under this title was pending with respect to a complaint or charge under this title based upon such discriminatory housing practice. This subparagraph does not apply to actions arising from a breach of a conciliation agreement.

(2) An aggrieved person may commence a civil action under this subsection whether or not a complaint has been filed under section 3610(a) and without regard to the status of any such complaint, but if the Secretary or a State or local agency has obtained a conciliation agreement with the consent of an aggrieved person, no action may be filed under this subsection by such aggrieved person with respect to the alleged discriminatory housing practice which forms the basis for such complaint except for the purpose of enforcing the terms of such an agreement.

(3) An aggrieved person may not commence a civil action under this subsection with respect to an alleged discriminatory housing practice which forms the basis of a charge issued by the Secretary if an administrative law judge has commenced a hearing on the record under this title with respect to such charge.

(b) Appointment of Attorney by Court.—

Upon application by a person alleging a discriminatory housing practice or a person against whom such a practice is alleged, the court may—

(1) appoint an attorney for such person; or

(2) authorize the commencement or continuation of a civil action under subsection (a) without the payment of fees, costs, or security, if in the opinion of the court such person is financially unable to bear the costs of such action.

(c) Relief Which May Be Granted.—

(1) In a civil action under subsection (a), if the court finds that a discriminatory housing practice has occurred or is about to occur, the court may award to the plaintiff actual and punitive damages, and subject to subsection (d), may grant as relief, as the court deems appropriate, any permanent or temporary injunction, temporary restraining order, or other order (including an order enjoining the defendant from engaging in such practice or ordering such affirmative action as may be appropriate).

(2) In a civil action under subsection (a), the court, in its discretion, may allow the prevailing party, other than the United States, a reason-

able attorney's fee and costs. The United States shall be liable for such fees and costs to the same extent as a private person.

(d) Effect on Certain Sales, Encumbrances, and Rentals.—

Relief granted under this section shall not affect any contract, sale, encumbrance, or lease consummated before the granting of such relief and involving a bona fide purchaser, encumbrancer, or tenant, without actual notice of the filing of a complaint with the Secretary or civil action under this subchapter.

(e) Intervention by Attorney General.—

Upon timely application, the Attorney General may intervene in such civil action, if the Attorney General certifies that the case is of general public importance. Upon such intervention the Attorney General may obtain such relief as would be available to the Attorney General under section 3614(e) in a civil action to which such section applies.

SEC. 3614. ENFORCEMENT BY THE ATTORNEY GENERAL

(a) Pattern or Practice Cases.—

Whenever the Attorney General has reasonable cause to believe that any person or group of persons is engaged in a pattern or practice of resistance to the full enjoyment of any of the rights granted by this subchapter, or that any group of persons has been denied any of the rights granted by this subchapter and such denial raises an issue of general public importance, the Attorney General may commence a civil action in any appropriate United States district court.

(b) On Referral of Discriminatory Housing Practice or Conciliation Agreement for Enforcement.—

(1)(A) The Attorney General may commence a civil action in any appropriate United States district court for appropriate relief with respect to a discriminatory housing practice referred to the Attorney General by the Secretary under section 810(g).

(B) A civil action under this paragraph may be commenced not later than the expiration of 18 months after the date of the occurrence or the termination of the alleged discriminatory housing practice.

(2)(A) The Attorney General may commence a civil action in any appropriate United States district court for appropriate relief with respect to breach of a conciliation agreement referred to the Attorney General by the Secretary under section 3610(c).

(B) A civil action may be commenced under this paragraph not later than the expiration of 90 days after the referral of the alleged breach under section 3610(c).

(c) Enforcement of Subpoenas.—

The Attorney General, on behalf of the Secretary, or other party at whose request a subpoena is issued, under this title, may enforce such subpoena in appropriate proceedings in the United States district court for the district in which the person to whom the subpoena was addressed resides, was served, or transacts business.

(d) Relief Which May Be Granted in Civil Actions Under Subsections (a) and (b).—

(1) In a civil action under subsection (a) or (b), the court—

(A) may award such preventive relief, including a permanent or temporary injunction, restraining order, or other order against the person responsible for a violation of this title as is necessary to assure the full enjoyment of the rights granted by this title;

(B) may award such other relief as the court deems appropriate, including monetary damages to persons aggrieved; and

(C) may, to vindicate the public interest, assess a civil penalty against the respondent—

(i) in an amount not exceeding $50,000, for a first violation; and

(ii) in an amount not exceeding $100,000, for any subsequent violation.

(2) In a civil action under this section, the court, in its discretion, may allow the prevailing party, other than the United States, a reasonable attorney's fee and costs. The United States shall be liable for such fees and costs to the extent provided by section 2412 of title 28.

(e) Intervention in Civil Actions.—

Upon timely application, any person may intervene in a civil action commenced by the Attorney General under subsection (a) or (b) of this section which involves an alleged discriminatory housing practice with respect to which such person is an aggrieved person or a conciliation agreement to which such person is a party. The court may grant such appropriate relief to any such intervening party as is authorized to be granted to a plaintiff in a civil action under section 3613 of this title.

SEC. 3614-1. INCENTIVES FOR SELF-TESTING AND SELF-CORRECTION

(a) Privileged Information.—

(1) Conditions For Privilege.— A report or result of a self-test (as that term is defined by regulation of the Secretary) shall be considered to be privileged under paragraph (2) if any person—

(A) conducts, or authorizes an independent third party to conduct, a self- test of any aspect of a residential real estate related lending transaction of that person, or any part of that transaction, in order to determine the level or effectiveness of compliance with this title by that person; and

(B) has identified any possible violation of this title by that person and has taken, or is taking, appropriate corrective action to address any such possible violation.

(2) Privileged Self-Test.— If a person meets the conditions specified in subparagraphs (A) and (B) of paragraph (1) with respect to a self-test described in that paragraph, any report or results of that self-test—

(A) shall be privileged; and

(B) may not be obtained or used by any applicant, department, or agency in any—

(i) proceeding or civil action in which one or more violations of this title are alleged; or

(ii) examination or investigation relating to compliance with this subchapter.

(b) Results of Self-Testing.—

(1) In General.— No provision of this section may be construed to prevent an aggrieved person, complainant, department, or agency from obtaining or using a report or results of any self-test in any proceeding or civil action in which a violation of this title is alleged, or in any examination or investigation of compliance with this subchapter if—

(A) the person to whom the self-test relates or any person with lawful access to the report or the results—

(i) voluntarily releases or discloses all, or any part of, the report or results to the aggrieved person, complainant, department, or agency, or to the general public; or

(ii) refers to or describes the report or results as a defense to charges of violations of this title against the person to whom the self-test relates; or

(B) the report or results are sought in conjunction with an adjudication or admission of a violation of this title for the sole purpose of determining an appropriate penalty or remedy.

(2) Disclosure for Determination of Penalty or Remedy.— Any report or results of a self-test that are disclosed for the purpose specified in paragraph (1)(B)—

(A) shall be used only for the particular proceeding in which the adjudication or admission referred to in paragraph (1)(B) is made; and

(B) may not be used in any other action or proceeding.

(c) Adjudication.—

An aggrieved person, complainant, department, or agency that challenges a privilege asserted under this section may seek a determination of the existence and application of that privilege in—

(1) a court of competent jurisdiction; or

(2) an administrative law proceeding with appropriate jurisdiction.

SEC. 3614A. RULES TO IMPLEMENT TITLE

The Secretary may make rules (including rules for the collection, maintenance, and analysis of appropriate data) to carry out this title. The Secretary shall give public notice and opportunity for comment with respect to all rules made under this section.

SEC. 3615. EFFECT ON STATE LAWS

Nothing in this subchapter shall be constructed to invalidate or limit any law of a State or political subdivision of a State, or of any other jurisdiction in which this subchapter shall be effective, that grants, guarantees, or protects the same rights as are granted by this subchapter; but any law of a State, a political subdivision, or other such jurisdiction that purports to require or permit any action that would be a discriminatory housing practice under this subchapter shall to that extent be invalid.

SEC. 3616. COOPERATION WITH STATE AND LOCAL AGENCIES ADMINISTERING FAIR HOUSING LAWS; UTILIZATION OF SERVICES AND PERSONNEL; REIMBURSEMENT; WRITTEN AGREEMENTS; PUBLICATION IN FEDERAL REGISTER

The Secretary may cooperate with State and local agencies charged with the administration of State and local fair housing laws and, with the consent of such agencies, utilize the services of such agencies and their employees and, notwithstanding any other provision of law, may reimburse such agencies and their employees for services rendered to assist him in carrying out this subchapter. In furtherance of such cooperative efforts, the Secretary may enter into written agreements with such State or local agencies. All agreements and terminations thereof shall be published in the Federal Register.

SECTION 3616A. FAIR HOUSING INITIATIVES PROGRAM

(a) In general

The Secretary of Housing and Urban Development (in this section referred to as the "Secretary") may make grants to, or (to the extent of amounts provided in appropriation Acts) enter into contracts or cooperative agreements with, State or local governments or their agencies, public or private nonprofit organizations or institutions, or other public or private entities that are formulating or carrying out programs to prevent or eliminate discriminatory housing practices, to develop, implement, carry out, or coordinate—

(1) programs or activities designed to obtain enforcement of the rights granted by title VIII of the Act of April 11, 1968 [42 U.S.C. 3601 et seq.] (commonly referred to as the Civil Rights Act of 1968), or by State or local laws that provide rights and remedies for alleged discriminatory housing practices that are substantially equivalent to the rights and remedies provided in such title VIII, through such appropriate judicial or administrative proceedings (including informal methods of conference, conciliation, and persuasion) as are available therefor; and

(2) education and outreach programs designed to inform the public concerning rights and obligations under the laws referred to in paragraph (1).

(b) Private enforcement initiatives

(1) In general

The Secretary shall use funds made available under this subsection to conduct, through contracts with private nonprofit fair housing enforcement organizations, investigations of violations of the rights granted under title VIII of the Civil Rights Act of 1968 [42 U.S.C. 3601 et seq.], and such enforcement activities as appropriate to remedy such violations. The Secretary may enter into multiyear contracts and take such other action as is appropriate to enhance the effectiveness of such investigations and enforcement activities.

(2) Activities

The Secretary shall use funds made available under this subsection to conduct, through contracts with private nonprofit fair housing enforcement organizations, a range of investigative and enforcement activities designed to—

(A) carry out testing and other investigative activities in accordance with subsection (b)(1) of this section, including building the capacity for housing investigative activities in unserved or underserved areas;

(B) discover and remedy discrimination in the public and private real estate markets and real estate-related transactions, including, but not limited to, the making or purchasing of loans or the provision of other financial assistance sales and rentals of housing and housing advertising;

(C) carry out special projects, including the development of prototypes to respond to new or sophisticated forms of discrimination against persons protected under title VIII of the Civil Rights Act of 1968 [42 U.S.C. 3601 et seq.];

(D) provide technical assistance to local fair housing organizations, and assist in the formation and development of new fair housing organizations; and

(E) provide funds for the costs and expenses of litigation, including expert witness fees.

(c) Funding of fair housing organizations

(1) In general

The Secretary shall use funds made available under this section to enter into contracts or cooperative agreements with qualified fair housing enforcement organizations, other private nonprofit fair housing enforcement organizations, and nonprofit groups organizing to build their capacity to provide fair housing enforcement, for the purpose of supporting the continued development or implementation of initiatives which enforce the rights granted under title VIII of the Civil Rights Act of 1968 [42 U.S.C. 3601 et seq.], as amended. Contracts or cooperative agreements may not provide more than 50 percent of the operating budget of the recipient organization for any one year.

(2) Capacity enhancement

The Secretary shall use funds made available under this section to help establish, organize, and build the capacity of fair housing enforcement organizations, particularly in those areas of the country which are currently underserved by fair housing enforcement organizations as well as those areas where large concentrations of protected classes exist. For purposes of meeting the objectives of this paragraph, the Secretary may enter into contracts or cooperative agreements with qualified fair housing enforcement organizations. The Secretary shall establish annual goals which reflect the national need for private fair housing enforcement organizations.

(d) Education and outreach

(1) In general

The Secretary, through contracts with one or more qualified fair housing enforcement organizations, other fair housing enforcement organizations, and other nonprofit organizations representing groups of persons protected under title VIII of the Civil Rights Act of 1968 [42 U.S.C. 3601 et seq.], shall establish a national education and outreach program. The national program shall be designed to provide a centralized, coordinated effort for the development and dissemination of fair housing media products, including—

(A) public service announcements, both audio and video;

(B) television, radio and print advertisements;

(C) posters; and

(D) pamphlets and brochures.

The Secretary shall designate a portion of the amounts provided in subsection (g)(4) of this section for a national program specifically for activities related to the annual national fair housing month. The Secretary shall encourage cooperation with real estate industry organizations in the national education and outreach program. The Secretary shall also encourage the dissemination of educational information and technical assistance to support compliance with the housing adaptability and accessibility guidelines contained in the Fair Housing Act Amendments of 1988.

(2) Regional and local programs

The Secretary, through contracts with fair housing enforcement organizations, other nonprofit organizations representing groups of persons protected under title VIII of the Civil Rights Act of 1968 [42 U.S.C. 3601 et seq.], State and local agencies certified by the Secretary under section 810(f) of the Fair Housing Act [42 U.S.C. 3610(f)], or other public or private entities that are formulating or carrying out programs to prevent or eliminate discriminatory housing practices, shall establish or support education and outreach programs at the regional and local levels.

(3) Community-based programs

The Secretary shall provide funding to fair housing organizations and other nonprofit organizations representing groups of persons protected under title VIII of the Civil Rights Act of 1968, or other public or private entities that are formulating or carrying out programs to prevent or eliminate discriminatory housing practices, to support community-based education and outreach activities, including school, church, and community presentations, conferences, and other educational activities.

(e) Program administration

(1) Not less than 30 days before providing a grant or entering into any contract or cooperative agreement to carry out activities authorized by this section, the Secretary shall submit notification of such proposed grant, contract, or cooperative agreement (including a description of the geographical distribution of such contracts) to the Committee on Banking, Housing, and Urban Affairs of the Senate and the Committee on Banking, Finance and Urban Affairs of the House of Representatives.

(2) Repealed. Pub. L. 104-66, title I, Sec. 1071(d), Dec. 21, 1995, 109 Stat. 720.

(f) Regulations

(1) The Secretary shall issue such regulations as may be necessary to carry out the provisions of this section.

(2) The Secretary shall, for use during the demonstration authorized in this section, establish guidelines for testing activities funded under the private enforcement initiative of the fair housing initiatives program. The purpose of such guidelines shall be to ensure that investigations in support of fair housing enforcement efforts described in subsection (a)(1) of this section shall develop credible and objective evidence of discriminatory housing practices. Such guidelines shall apply only to activities funded under this section, shall not be construed to limit or otherwise restrict the use of facts secured through testing not funded under this section in any legal proceeding under Federal fair housing laws, and shall not be used to restrict individuals or entities, including those participating in the fair housing initiatives program, from pursuing any right or remedy guaranteed by Federal law. Not later than 6 months after the end of the demonstration period authorized in this section, the Secretary shall submit to Congress the evaluation of the Secretary of the effectiveness of such guidelines in achieving the purposes of this section.

(3) Such regulations shall include provisions governing applications for assistance under this section, and shall require each such application to contain—

(A) a description of the assisted activities proposed to be undertaken by the applicant, together with the estimated costs and schedule for completion of such activities;

(B) a description of the experience of the applicant in formulating or carrying out programs to prevent or eliminate discriminatory housing practices;

(C) available information, including studies made by or available to the applicant, indicating the nature and extent of discriminatory housing practices occurring in the general location where the applicant proposes to conduct its assisted activities, and the relationship of such activities to such practices;

(D) an estimate of such other public or private resources as may be available to assist the proposed activities;

(E) a description of proposed procedures to be used by the applicant for monitoring conduct and evaluating results of the proposed activities; and

(F) any additional information required by the Secretary.

(4) Regulations issued under this subsection shall not become effective prior to the expiration of 90 days after the Secretary transmits such regulations, in the form such regulations are intended to be published, to the Committee on Banking, Housing, and Urban Affairs of the Senate and the Committee on Banking, Finance and Urban Affairs of the House of Representatives.

(5) The Secretary shall not obligate or expend any amount under this section before the effective date of the regulations required under this subsection.

(g) Authorization of appropriations

There are authorized to be appropriated to carry out the provisions of this section, $21,000,000 for fiscal year 1993 and $26,000,000 for fiscal year 1994, of which—

(1) not less than $3,820,000 for fiscal year 1993 and $8,500,000 for fiscal year 1994 shall be for private enforcement initiatives authorized under subsection (b) of this section, divided equally between activities specified under subsection (b)(1) of this section and those specified under subsection (b)(2) of this section;

(2) not less than $2,230,000 for fiscal year 1993 and $8,500,000 for fiscal year 1994 shall be for qualified fair housing enforcement organizations authorized under subsection (c)(1) of this section;

(3) not less than $2,010,000 for fiscal year 1993 and $4,000,000 for fiscal year 1994 shall be for the creation of new fair housing enforcement organizations authorized under subsection (c)(2) of this section; and

(4) not less than $2,540,000 for fiscal year 1993 and $5,000,000 for fiscal year 1994 shall be for education and outreach programs authorized under subsection (d) of thia section, to be divided equally between activities specified under subsection (d)(1) of this section and those specified under subsections (d)(2) and (d)(3) of this section.

Any amount appropriated under this section shall remain available until expended.

(h) Qualified fair housing enforcement organization

(1) The term "qualified fair housing enforcement organization" means any organization that—

(A) is organized as a private, tax-exempt, nonprofit, charitable organization;

(B) has at least 2 years experience in complaint intake, complaint investigation, testing for fair housing violations and enforcement of meritorious claims; and

(C) is engaged in all the activities listed in paragraph (1)(B) at the time of application for assistance under this section.

An organization which is not solely engaged in fair housing enforcement activities may qualify as a qualified fair housing enforcement organization, provided that the organization is actively engaged in each of the activities listed in subparagraph (B).

(2) The term "fair housing enforcement organization" means any organization that—

(A) meets the requirements specified in paragraph (1)(A);

(B) is currently engaged in the activities specified in paragraph (1)(B);

(C) upon the receipt of funds under this section will become engaged in all of the activities specified in paragraph (1)(B); and

(D) for purposes of funding under subsection (b) of this section, has at least 1 year of experience in the activities specified in paragraph (1)(B).

(i) Prohibition on use of funds

None of the funds authorized under this section may be used by the Secretary for purposes of settling claims, satisfying judgments or fulfilling court orders in any litigation action involving either the Department or housing providers funded by the Department. None of the funds authorized under this section may be used by the Department for administrative costs.

(j) Reporting requirements

Not later than 180 days after the close of each fiscal year in which assistance under this section is furnished, the Secretary shall prepare and submit to the Congress a comprehensive report which shall contain—

(1) a description of the progress made in accomplishing the objectives of this section;

(2) a summary of all the private enforcement activities carried out under this section and the use of such funds during the preceding fiscal year;

(3) a list of all fair housing enforcement organizations funded under this section during the preceding fiscal year, identified on a State-by-State basis;

(4) a summary of all education and outreach activities funded under this section and the use of such funds during the preceding fiscal year; and

(5) any findings, conclusions, or recommendations of the Secretary as a result of the funded activities.

SEC. 3617. INTERFERENCE, COERCION, OR INTIMIDATION; ENFORCEMENT BY CIVIL ACTION

It shall be unlawful to coerce, intimidate, threaten, or interfere with any person in the exercise or enjoyment of, or on account of his having exercised or enjoyed, or on account of his having aided or encouraged any other person in the exercise or enjoyment of, any right granted or protected by section 3603, 3604, 3605, or 3606 of this title.

SEC. 3618. AUTHORIZATION OF APPROPRIATIONS

There are hereby authorized to be appropriated such sums as are necessary to carry out the purposes of this subchapter.

SEC. 3619. SEPARABILITY OF PROVISIONS

If any provision of this subchapter or the application thereof to any person or circumstances is held invalid, the remainder of the subchapter and the application of the provision to other persons not similarly situated or to other circumstances shall not be affected thereby.

SEC. 3631. VIOLATIONS; PENALTIES

Whoever, whether or not acting under color of law, by force or threat of force willfully injures, intimidates or interferes with or attempts to injure, intimidate or interfere with—

(a) any person because of his race, color, religion, sex, handicap (as such term is defined in section 3602 of this title) familial status (as such term is defined in section 3602 of this title), or national origin and because he is or has been selling, purchasing, renting, financing, occupying, or contracting or negotiating for the sale, purchase, rental, financing or occupation of any dwelling, or applying for or participating in any service, organization, or facility relating to the business of selling or renting dwellings; or

(b) any person because he is or has been, or in order to intimidate such person or any other person or any class of persons from—

(1) participating, without discrimination on account of race, color, religion, sex, handicap (as such term is defined in section 3602 of this title), familial status (as such term is defined in section 3602 of this title), or national origin, in any of the activities, services, organizations or facilities described in subsection (a) of this section; or

(2) affording another person or class of persons opportunity or protection so to participate; or

(c) any citizen because he is or has been, or in order to discourage such citizen or any other citizen from lawfully aiding or encouraging other persons to participate, without discrimination on account of race, color, religion, sex, handicap (as such term is defined in section 3602 of this title), familial status (as such term is defined in section 3602 of this title), or national origin, in any of the activities, services, organizations or facilities described in subsection (a) of this section, or participating lawfully in speech or peaceful assembly opposing any denial of the opportunity to so participate shall be fined under title 18 or imprisoned not more than one year, or both; and if bodily injury results from the acts committed in violation of this section or if such acts include the use, attempted use, or threatened use of a dangerous weapon, explosives, or fire shall be fined under title 18 or imprisoned not more than ten years, or both; and if death results from the acts committed in violation of this section or if such acts include kidnapping or an attempt to kidnap, aggravated sexual abuse or an attempt to commit aggravated sexual abuse, or an attempt to kill, shall be fined under title 18 or imprisoned for any term of years or for life, or both.

APPENDIX 6:
HUD FAIR HOUSING DISCRIMINATION COMPLAINT FORM

OMB Approval No. 2529-0011 (expires 11/30/2007)

U.S. Department of Housing and Urban Development
Office of Fair Housing and Equal Opportunity

Are you a Victim of Housing Discrimination?

Fair Housing is Your Right!

If you have been denied your housing rights ... you may have experienced housing discrimination.

How do you recognize Housing Discrimination?

Under the Fair Housing Act, It is Against the Law to:

- Refuse to rent to you or sell you housing
- Tell you housing is unavailable when in fact it is available
- Show you apartments or homes in certain neighborhoods only
- Advertise housing to preferred groups of people only
- Refuse to provide you with information regarding mortgage loans, deny you a mortgage loan, or impose different terms or conditions on a mortgage loan
- Deny you property insurance
- Conduct property appraisals in a discriminatory manner
- Refuse to make certain modifications or accommodations for persons with a mental or physical disability, including persons recovering from alcohol and substance abuse, and HIV/AIDS-related illnesses
- Fail to design and construct housing in an accessible manner
- Harass, coerce, intimidate, or interfere with anyone exercising or assisting someone else with their fair housing rights

Based on these factors...

- Race
- Color
- National origin
- Religion
- Sex
- Familial status (families with children under the age of 18, or who are expecting a child), or
- Handicap (if you or someone close to you has a disability)

If you don't report discrimination, it can't be stopped!

Housing Discrimination Information Form

- If you believe your rights have been violated, HUD or a State or local fair housing agency is ready to help you file a complaint.

- You have one year from the date of the alleged act of discrimination to file your complaint.

- After your information is received, we will contact you to discuss the concerns you raise.

Instructions: (Please type or print.) Read this form carefully. Try to answer all questions. If you do not know the answer or a question does not apply to you, leave the space blank. You have one year from the date of the alleged discrimination to file a complaint. Your form should be signed and dated. Use reverse side of this page if you need more space to respond.

Keep this information for your records.

Date you mailed your information to HUD:(mm/dd/yyyy)

Address to which you sent the information:
Street:

City: State: Zip Code:

If you have not heard from HUD or a fair housing agency within three weeks from the date you mail this form, you may call to inquire about the status of your complaint. See addresses and telephone listings on the last page.

Your Name:	Best time to call:	Your Daytime Phone No:
Your Address:		Evening Phone No:
City:	State:	Zip Code:

Who else can we call if we cannot reach you?

1 Contact's Name:	Daytime Phone No:
Best time to call:	Evening Phone No:
2 Contact's Name:	Daytime Phone No:
Best time to call:	Evening Phone No:

1. **What** happened to you? How were you discriminated against? For example: were you refused an opportunity to rent or buy housing? Denied a loan? Told that housing was not available when in fact it was? Treated differently from others seeking housing? State briefly what happened.

2. **Why** do you believe you are being discriminated against?

It is a violation of the law to deny you your housing rights for any of the following factors: • race • color • religion • sex • national origin • familial status (families with children under 18) • disability.

For example: were you denied housing **because of** your race? Were you denied a mortgage loan **because of** your religion? Or turned down for an apartment **because** you have children? Were you harassed because you assisted someone in obtaining their fair housing rights? Briefly explain why you think your housing rights were denied **because of** any the factors listed above.

3. **Who** do you believe discriminated against you? Was it a landlord, owner, bank, real estate agent, broker, company, or organization?

Name:

Address:

4. **Where** did the alleged act of discrimination occur? Provide the address. For example: Was it at a rental unit? Single family home? Public or Assisted Housing? A Mobile Home? Did it occur at a bank or other lending institution?

Address:

City: State: Zip Code:

5. **When** did the last act of discrimination occur?
Enter the date (mm/dd/yyyy) _____
Is the alleged discrimination continuous or on going? ☐ Yes ☐ No

Signature: Date:(mm/dd/yyyy)

X _____

Send this form to HUD or to the fair housing agency where the alleged act of discrimination occurred.
If you are unable to complete this form, you may call the office nearest you.
See addresses and telephone numbers listed on the back page.

Previous Versions Obsolete   Page 5 of 7   form **HUD-903.1** (7/2004)

The information collected here will be used to investigate and to process housing discrimination complaints. The information may be disclosed to the United States Department of Justice for its use in the filing of pattern and practice suits of housing discrimination or the prosecution of the person(s) who committed the discrimination where violence is involved; and to State or local fair housing agencies that administer substantially equivalent fair housing laws for complaint processing.

Public Reporting Burden for this collection of information is estimated to average 20 minutes per response, including the time for reviewing instructions, searching existing data sources, gathering and maintaining the data needed, and completing and reviewing the collection of information.

Disclosure of this information is voluntary. Failure to provide some or all of the requested information will result in delay or denial of HUD assistance.

This agency may not collect this information, and you are not required to complete this form, unless it displays a currently valid OMB control number.

Privacy Act Statement The Department of Housing and Urban Development is authorized to collect this information by Title VIII of the Civil Rights Act of 1968, as amended by the Fair Housing Amendments Act of 1988, (P.L. 100-430); Title VI of the Civil Rights Act of 1964, (P.L. 88-352); Section 504 of the Rehabilitation Act of 1973, as amended, (P.L. 93-112); Section 109 of Title I - Housing and Community Development Act of 1974, as amended, (P.L. 97-35); Americans with Disabilities Act of 1990, (P.L. 101-336); and by the Age Discrimination Act of 1975, as amended, (42 U.S.C. 6103).

For Connecticut, Maine, Massachusetts, New Hampshire, Rhode Island, and Vermont:

NEW ENGLAND OFFICE
(Marcella_Brown@hud.gov)

Fair Housing Enforcement Center
U.S. Department of Housing and Urban Development
Thomas P. O'Neill, Jr. Federal Building
10 Causeway Street, Room 321
Boston, MA 02222-1092
Telephone (617) 994-8300 or 1-800-827-5005
Fax (617) 565-7313 • TTY (617) 565-5453

For New Jersey and New York

New York/New Jersey Office
(Stanley_Seidenfeld@hud.gov)
Fair Housing Enforcement Center
U.S. Department of Housing and Urban Development
26 Federal Plaza, Room 3532
New York, NY 10278-0068
Telephone (212) 264-1290 or 1-800-496-4294
Fax (212) 264-9829 • TTY (212) 264-0927

For Delaware, District of Columbia, Maryland, Pennsylvania, Virginia, and West Virginia

MID-ATLANTIC OFFICE
(Wanda_Nieves@hud.gov)
Fair Housing Enforcement Center
U.S. Department of Housing and Urban Development
The Wanamaker Building
100 Penn Square East
Philadelphia, PA 19107-9344
Telephone (215) 656-0662 or 1-888-799-2085
Fax (215) 656-3419 • TTY (215) 656-3450

For Alabama, the Caribbean, Florida, Georgia, Kentucky, Mississippi, North Carolina, South Carolina, and Tennessee:

SOUTHEAST/CARIBBEAN OFFICE
(Gregory_L._King@hud.gov)
Fair Housing Enforcement Center
U.S. Department of Housing and Urban Development
Five Points Plaza
40 Marietta Street, 16th Floor
Atlanta, GA 30303-2806
Telephone (404) 331-5140 or 1-800-440-8091
Fax (404) 331-1021 • TTY (404) 730-2654

For Illinois, Indiana, Michigan, Minnesota, Ohio, and Wisconsin:

MIDWEST OFFICE
(Barbara_Knox@hud.gov)
Fair Housing Enforcement Center
U.S. Department of Housing and Urban Development
Ralph H. Metcalfe Federal Building
77 West Jackson Boulevard, Room 2101
Chicago, IL 60604-3507
Telephone (312) 353-7776 or 1-800-765-9372
Fax (312) 886-2837 • TTY (312) 353-7143

For Arkansas, Louisiana, New Mexico, Oklahoma, and Texas:

SOUTHWEST OFFICE
(Thurman_G._Miles@hud.gov or Garry_L._Sweeney@hud.gov)
Fair Housing Enforcement Center
U.S. Department of Housing and Urban Development
801 North Cherry, 27th Floor
Fort Worth, TX 76102
Telephone (817) 978-5900 or 1-888-560-8913
Fax (817) 978-5876 or 5851 • TTY (817) 978-5595

For Iowa, Kansas, Missouri and Nebraska:

GREAT PLAINS OFFICE
(Robbie_Herndon@hud.gov)

Fair Housing Enforcement Center
U.S. Department of Housing and
Urban Development
Gateway Tower II
400 State Avenue, Room 200, 4th
Floor
Kansas City, KS 66101-2406
Telephone (913) 551-6958 or
1-800-743-5323
Fax (913) 551-6856 • TTY (913)
551-6972

For Colorado, Montana, North Dakota, South Dakota, Utah, and Wyoming:

ROCKY MOUNTAINS OFFICE
(Sharon_L._Santoya@hud.gov)

Fair Housing Enforcement Center
U.S. Department of Housing and
Urban Development
633 17th Street
Denver, CO 80202-3690
Telephone (303) 672-5437 or
1-800-877-7353
Fax (303) 672-5026 • TTY (303)
672-5248

For Arizona, California, Hawaii, and Nevada:

PACIFIC/HAWAII OFFICE
(Charles_Hauptman@hud.gov)

Fair Housing Enforcement Center
U.S. Department of Housing and
Urban Development
600 Harrison Street, 3rd Floor
San Francisco, CA 94107-1300
Telephone (415) 489-6524 or
1-800-347-3739
Fax (415) 489-6559 • TTY (415)
489-6564

For Alaska, Idaho, Oregon, and Washington:

NORTHWEST/ALASKA OFFICE
(Judith_Keeler@hud.gov)

Fair Housing Enforcement Center
U.S. Department of Housing and
Urban Development
Seattle Federal Office Building
909 First Avenue, Room 205
Seattle, WA 98104-1000
Telephone (206) 220-5170 or
1-800-877-0246
Fax (206) 220-5447 • TTY (206)
220-5185

If after contacting the local office nearest you, you still have questions – you may contact HUD further at:

U.S. Department of Housing and
Urban Development
Office of Fair Housing and Equal
Opportunity
451 7th Street, S.W., Room 5204
Washington, DC 20410-2000
Telephone (202) 708-0836 or
1-800-669-9777
Fax (202) 708-1425 • TTY 1-800-
927-9275

Previous Versions Obsolete   Page 7 of 7   form **HUD-903.1** (7/2004)

Your Rights as a Tenant   139

APPENDIX 7:
SAMPLE LEASE

LEASE

This Agreement is made on [insert date] between [Landlord Name and Address] and [Tenant Name and Address] upon the following terms and conditions:

I. PREMISES TO BE LEASED

1. Rental Property Address:

2. Description of Rental Property: [e.g., 1 bedroom/1 bath]

3. Inclusions: [e.g., furnishings, heat/hot water, etc.]

4. Exclusions: [e.g., electricity, air conditioning, etc.]

5. Condition of Property: Landlord has [#] days after lease signing to provide tenant with a complete inspection condition checklist. Tenant then has [#] additional days to inspect the premises and agree or disagree with landlord's checklist.

II. LEASE TERMS

1. Commencement Date of Lease:

2. End Date of Lease:

3. Lease Term: [e.g., 2 years]

III. RENT

1. Monthly Rent:

2. Due Date: Rent is to be paid on the ____ day of each month as follows: [Insert Payment Address]

3. Late Charges: In the event the rent is not paid by the due date, a late charge in the amount of [Insert Amount] will be assessed.

IV. SECURITY DEPOSIT

1. Amount of Security Deposit:

2. Tenant's security deposit will be held in an interest bearing account with the following bank: [Insert Bank Name and Address]

3. Landlord must make reasonable efforts to give tenant notice of their right to be present at the time landlord conducts an end of lease inspection of the rental property. Tenant must then make a written request to landlord to be present at such inspection. If tenant makes no written request or fails to schedule or appear at any scheduled inspection, landlord will perform the inspection without the presence of tenant.

4. Landlord has [# days] after the end of the lease term to return the tenant's security deposit, along with any accrued interest. If landlord intends to withhold all or a portion of tenant's security deposit, landlord must give tenant a written statement as to why such funds are being withheld. Landlord must provide tenant with an itemized list of all deductions from the security deposit.

5. Landlord may apply all or a portion of the tenant's security deposit to rental property damages; however no portion of the security deposit will be withheld from tenant due to normal wear and tear resulting from ordinary use of the rental premises.

6. Landlord may apply all or a portion of any remaining security deposit to the payment of accumulated rent, unpaid charges, and legal fees and costs, if applicable.

7. If landlord's damages exceed the amount of the security deposit, a third-party contractor may be needed and landlord must provide written notice to tenant within 30 days after the lease term ends. If notice is given, landlord shall have an additional 15 days to provide tenant with a detailed description of such additional damages and the cost of repairs.

8. Tenant may not apply any portion of the security deposit towards the final month's rent payment.

V. MAINTENANCE AND REPAIRS

1. Landlord is responsible for maintaining the common areas of the landlord's premises in accordance with state and local law.

2. Tenant is responsible for maintaining the rental property and will be held liable for any damages caused to the rental property that are not considered normal wear and tear.

3. Tenant must give landlord written notice of any items that need to be repaired in the rental property.

4. There should be no substantial property alterations, including additions and improvement, without the prior written consent of the landlord. In any event, at termination of the lease the tenant must restore the premises to its condition at the beginning of the tenancy.

VI. SUBLET AND ASSIGNMENT

Tenant is prohibited from assigning this lease or subletting the rental property without prior written consent from the landlord.

VII. PETS

Tenant is prohibited from housing any pets in the rental property.

VIII. KEYS

Landlord will determine the number of keys given to tenant, the cost of lost keys, and the cost of reentering the property if the tenant is locked out of the rental property.

VIX. DESTRUCTION OF PREMISES

In the event the rental property is partially or completely destroyed, either party may terminate this agreement upon [#] days' written notice.

X. QUIET ENJOYMENT OF PREMISES

1. Landlord will try to the best of his or her abilities to afford tenant quiet enjoyment of the rental property.

2. Tenant agrees to use the rental property in a quiet, peaceable, lawful and residential manner.

XI. LEASE TERMINATION

In the case of a termination of the lease, the tenant is to vacate the premises, return all keys, remove all personal property, and leave the property in its pre-rental condition, except for normal wear and tear.

XII. LEASE AMENDMENTS

This lease may be amended, in writing, with the written approval of both parties obligated by this agreement.

SIGNATURE LINE – LANDLORD

SIGNATURE LINE – TENANT

NOTE: The rental property described above shall be made available to all with no regard to race, color, creed, nationality, religion, sex, sexual orientation, familial status, handicap, or age in compliance with federal, state, and local fair housing laws.

APPENDIX 8:
LEASE - SHORT FORM

THIS AGREEMENT, is made this ____ date of _____, 20__, between [Name of Landlord] ("Landlord") and [Name of Tenant] ("Tenant").

For good and valuable consideration, it is agreed between the above-named parties as follows:

1. Landlord hereby leases and lets to Tenant the premises described as follows: [Insert address of property being leased].

2. This Lease shall be for a term of [Insert term, e.g., # years, # months, etc.] , commencing on [Commencement Date] and terminating on [Termination Date] .

3. Tenant shall pay Landlord the rent of [Specify dollar amount and manner in which payments are to be made, e.g., Fifteen Hundred Dollars per month, payable on the first day of each month in advance].

4. Tenant shall pay a security deposit of [Dollar Amount ($xxx)] Dollars, which amount shall be held in an interest-bearing account in [Name and Address of Bank], to be returned upon termination of this lease and full performance of all obligations hereunder, including the payment of all rent due.

5. Tenant shall at his/her own expense provide the following utilities: [Specify which utilities Tenant shall be liable for, e.g., electricity, gas, water, etc.].

6. Landlord shall at his/her own expense provide the following utilities: [Specify which utilities Landlord shall be liable for, e.g., electricity, gas, water, etc.].

7. Tenant further agrees that upon the termination of the Lease Tenant will return possession of the leased premises in its present condi-

tion, reasonable wear and tear excepted. Further, Tenant shall commit no waste to the leased premises.

8. Tenant shall not assign or sublet said premises or allow any other person to occupy the leased premises without Landlord's prior written consent, which consent shall not be unreasonably withheld.

9. Tenant shall not make any material or structural alterations to the leased premises without Landlord's prior written consent.

10. Tenant shall comply with all building, zoning and health codes and other applicable laws for the use of said leased premises.

11. Tenant shall not conduct on premises hazardous activities, or activities deemed a nuisance.

12. Tenant shall not allow pets on the premises [alternative language: except those specifically set forth herein].

13. In the event of any breach of the payment of rent or other breach of this Lease, Landlord shall have full rights to terminate this Lease in accordance with the applicable state law, and enter and reclaim possession of the leased premises, in addition to any other remedies available to Landlord arising from said breach.

14. This Lease shall be binding upon and inure to the benefit of the parties, their successors, assigns and personal representatives.

15. This Lease shall be subordinate to all present or future mortgages against the property.

16. [Set forth any additional terms agreed to between the parties].

BY: _____ _____

    [SIGNATURE LINE - LANDLORD]

BY: _____

    [SIGNATURE LINE - TENANT]

APPENDIX 9:
LEASE ARBITRATION CLAUSE

It is hereby agreed by and between the parties to the Lease, that if at any time during the term of the Lease there shall arise a dispute relating to any provision of said Lease, or to the rights and responsibilities of the parties to said Lease, such dispute shall be submitted to the American Arbitration Association for a determination of the dispute, and the parties agree that said determination shall be binding upon the parties.

APPENDIX 10:
SUBLEASE

THIS AGREEMENT, is made this ___ day of _____, 20__, between [Name of Landlord] ("Landlord") and [Name of Tenant] ("Tenant"), and [Name of Subtenant] ("Subtenant").

For good and valuable consideration, it is agreed between the above-named parties as follows:

1. The Tenant agrees to sublease to the Subtenant the premises described as follows: [Insert address of property being leased].

2. The Subtenant agrees to comply with all terms and conditions of the original lease entered into between Tenant and Landlord on [Insert Date of Original Lease], including the prompt payment of all rents. Those lease terms are incorporated into this agreement by reference.

3. The Subtenant agrees to pay the Landlord the monthly rent stated in that lease, and all other rental charges hereinafter due, and otherwise assume all of Tenant's obligations during the Sublease period and indemnify Tenant from same.

4. The Subtenant agrees to pay to Tenant the sum of [Dollar Amount ($xxx)] Dollars as a security deposit, to be promptly returned upon the termination of this sublease and compliance of all its conditions.

5. Attached to this agreement is an inventory of items or fixtures located on the above described property as of [Insert Date] . The Subtenant agrees to replace or reimburse the Tenant for any of these items that are missing or damaged at the time Tenant takes repossession of the premises.

6. The Landlord consents to this sublease and agrees to promptly notify the Tenant if the Subtenant is in breach of this agreement.

7. Nothing herein shall constitute a release of Tenant who shall remain bound under the original lease.

8. Nothing herein shall constitute a consent to any further Sublease or Assignment of Lease.

9. [Set forth any additional terms agreed to between the parties].

BY: _____
    [SIGNATURE LINE - LANDLORD]

BY: _____
    [SIGNATURE LINE - TENANT]

IN THE PRESENCE OF:

BY: _____
    [SIGNATURE LINE - WITNESS]

APPENDIX 11:
RULES FOR RETURNING SECURITY
DEPOSITS, BY STATE

STATE	DEADLINE
Alabama	No statutory deadline
Alaska	14 days if the tenant gives proper notice to terminate tenancy; 30 days if the tenant does not give proper notice
Arizona	14 days
Arkansas	30 days
California	Three weeks
Colorado	One month, unless lease agreement specifies longer period of time, which may be no more than 60 days; 72 hours, not counting weekends or holidays, if a hazardous condition involving gas equipment requires tenant to vacate
Connecticut	30 days, or within 15 days of receiving tenant's forwarding address, whichever is later
Delaware	20 days
District of Columbia	45 days
Florida	15 to 60 days depending on whether tenant disputes deductions
Georgia	One month
Hawaii	14 days
Idaho	21 days or up to 30 days if landlord and tenant agree
Illinois	30-45 days depending on whether tenant disputes deductions
Indiana	45 days
Iowa	30 days
Kansas	30 days
Kentucky	30-60 days depending on whether tenant disputes deductions
Louisiana	One month
Maine	30 days if written rental agreement; 21 days if tenancy at will
Maryland	30-45 days depending on whether tenant has been evicted or has abandoned the premises

STATE	DEADLINE
Massachusetts	30 days
Michigan	30 days
Minnesota	Three weeks after tenant leaves and landlord receives mailing address; five days if tenant must leave due to building condemnation
Mississippi	45 days
Missouri	30 days
Montana	30 days; 10 days if no deductions
Nebraska	14 days
Nevada	30 days
New Hampshire	30 days; for shared facilities, if the deposit is more than 30 days' rent, landlord must provide written agreement acknowledging receipt and specifying when deposit will be returned; if no written agreement, 20 days after tenant vacates
New Jersey	30 days; five days in case of fire, flood, condemnation, or evacuation
New Mexico	30 days
New York	Reasonable time
North Carolina	30 days
North Dakota	30 days
Ohio	30 days
Oklahoma	30 days
Oregon	31 days
Pennsylvania	30 days
Rhode Island	20 days
South Carolina	30 days
South Dakota	Two weeks to return entire deposit or a portion and supply reasons for withholding; 45 days for a written, itemized accounting if tenant requests it
Tennessee	No statutory deadline
Texas	30 days
Utah	30 days, or within 15 days of receiving tenant's forwarding address, whichever is later
Vermont	14 days
Virginia	45 days
Washington	14 days
West Virginia	No statutory deadline
Wisconsin	21 days

APPENDIX 12:
WARRANTY OF HABITABILITY - NEW YORK STATE

ARTICLE 7 - Landlord and Tenant

SECTION 235-b. Warranty of habitability.

1. In every written or oral lease or rental agreement for residential premises the landlord or lessor shall be deemed to covenant and warrant that the premises so leased or rented and all areas used in connection therewith in common with other tenants or residents are fit for human habitation and for the uses reasonably intended by the parties and that the occupants of such premises shall not be subjected to any conditions which would be dangerous, hazardous or detrimental to their life, health or safety. When any such condition has been caused by the misconduct of the tenant or lessee or persons under his direction or control, it shall not constitute a breach of such covenants and warranties.

2. Any agreement by a lessee or tenant of a dwelling waiving or modifying his rights as set forth in this section shall be void as contrary to public policy.

3. In determining the amount of damages sustained by a tenant as a result of a breach of the warranty set forth in the section, the court;

    (a) need not require any expert testimony; and

    (b) shall, to the extent the warranty is breached or cannot be cured by reason of a strike or other labor dispute which is not caused primarily by the individual landlord or lessor and such damages are attributable to such strike, exclude recovery to such extent, except to the extent of the net savings, if any, to the landlord or lessor by reason of such strike or labor dispute allocable to the tenant's premises, provided, however, that the landlord or lesser has made a good faith attempt, where practicable, to cure the breach.

APPENDIX 13:
COMPLAINT BY TENANT FOR BREACH OF
WARRANTY OF HABITABILITY

CAPTION OF CASE

COMPLAINT

Plaintiff, JOHN SMITH, residing at [Address], by his attorney, [Attorney Name], as and for his Complaint against the defendant [Name of Landlord], with offices located at [Address], alleges as follows:

1. At all times hereinafter mentioned, plaintiff was a resident of the County of [County Name], State of [State Name].

2. At all times hereinafter mentioned, defendant was a resident of the County of [County Name], State of [State Name].

3. At all times hereinafter mentioned, defendant was the owner of a residential apartment building located at [Address of Rental Property].

4. At all times hereinafter mentioned, plaintiff was a tenant of the defendant, and occupied an apartment known as [Unit #], located on the [#] floor of said apartment building.

5. At all times hereinafter mentioned, the defendant breached its warranty of habitability of the leased premises in that [describe circumstances, e.g., the ceiling tiles located in the living room of said apartment were loose], and that this condition had been in existence prior to the occurrence herein complained of, and that defendant had actual and constructive knowledge of this problem.

6. On _____, 20__, plaintiff was sitting in his living room when [describe damages, e.g., one of the ceiling tiles fell on his head, causing him to suffer severe injuries to his head and neck, all or some of which may be permanent].

7. Said injuries were caused by the failure of defendant to properly maintain the premises, and defendant's breach of warranty of habitability of the leased premises.

8. The plaintiff in no way contributed to his injuries.

WHEREFORE, plaintiff seeks judgment against the defendant in the sum of [($) Dollar Amount] Dollars, together with the costs and disbursements of this action, and for such other and further relief as the Court deems proper.

BY: _____

      NAME OF ATTORNEY

      ATTORNEY FOR PLAINTIFF

      OFFICE ADDRESS

      TELEPHONE NUMBER

APPENDIX 14:
COVENANT OF QUIET ENJOYMENT OF LEASED PREMISES

Landlord hereby covenants, warrants and represents to Tenant that, upon payment of the rent and observing all provisions herein required by this Lease, Tenant shall have the right to quietly and peaceably have, hold and enjoy the premises during the term set forth in the Lease.

APPENDIX 15:
NOTICE TO LANDLORD OF TENANT'S INTENTION TO VACATE LEASED PREMISES

[DATE OF NOTICE]

[VIA CERTIFIED MAIL – RETURN RECEIPT REQUESTED]

Landlord's Name

Street Address

City, State Zip Code

RE: Notice of Intention to Vacate Leased Premises Located at [Insert Premises Address]

As set forth in our lease dated [Insert Date of Lease], I hereby notify you of my intention to vacate the above-referenced premises on [Insert Date]. Please forward the security deposit to me in care of the following address:

[Tenant's Forwarding Address]

BY: _____

[SIGNATURE LINE - TENANT]

APPENDIX 16:
30-DAY EVICTION NOTICE

30 DAY EVICTION NOTICE

TO: [Tenant's Name and Address]

YOU ARE HEREBY NOTIFIED THAT your tenancy in the premises situated in the City of [Tenant's City], County of [Tenant's County], and State of [Tenant's State], being described as follows: [Tenant's Street Address] shall be terminated as of [Date of Termination].

Demand is hereby made that you vacate the said premises and deliver up possession thereof to the undersigned at that time. No further demand shall be necessary before bringing legal proceedings to recover the premises.

Dated this ____ of _____, 20__.

BY: _____

    [SIGNATURE LINE]

APPENDIX 17:
THREE-DAY NOTICE TO TENANT TO VACATE THE LEASED PREMISES DUE TO NON-PAYMENT OF RENT

[DATE OF NOTICE]

[VIA CERTIFIED MAIL – RETURN RECEIPT REQUESTED]

Tenant's Name

Street Address

City, State Zip Code

RE: Three-Day Notice to Vacate Leased Premises Located at [Insert Premises Address] for Non-Payment of Rent

You are hereby notified to surrender the above-referenced leased premises you occupy as our tenant and to vacate said premises on or within three days of your receipt of this notice, as a consequence of your non-payment of rent due under the lease.

The present rent due and owing in connection with said lease is [($) Dollar Amount] Dollars. This notice may be rescinded upon full payment of said amount within three days of your receipt of this notice.

If you fail to pay all rent payments due and owing, we will have no recourse but to seek immediate legal action to evict you from said premises and to seek damages and attorneys' fees and costs as prescribed by law.

BY: _____

    [SIGNATURE LINE - LANDLORD]

APPENDIX 18:
UNIFORM RESIDENTIAL LANDLORD AND TENANT ACT

ARTICLE I: GENERAL PROVISIONS AND DEFINITIONS

PART I. SHORT TITLE, CONSTRUCTION, APPLICATION AND SUBJECT MATTER OF THE ACT

§ 1.101. [Short Title]

This Act shall be known and may be cited as the "Uniform Residential Landlord and Tenant Act."

§ 1.102. [Purposes; Rules of Construction]

(a) This Act shall be liberally construed and applied to promote its underlying purposes and policies.

(b) Underlying purposes and policies of this Act are

(1) to simplify, clarify, modernize, and revise the law governing the rental of dwelling units and the rights and obligations of landlords and tenants;

(2) to encourage landlords and tenants to maintain and improve the quality of housing; and

(3) to make uniform the law with respect to the subject of this Act among those states which enact it.

§ 1.103. [Supplementary Principles of Law Applicable]

Unless displaced by the provisions of this Act, the principles of law and equity, including the law relating to capacity to contract, mutuality of obligations, principal and agent, real property, public health, safety and fire prevention, estoppel, fraud, misrepresentation, duress, coercion, mistake, bankruptcy, or other validating or invalidating cause supplement its provisions.

§ 1.104. [Construction Against Implicit Repeal]

This Act being a general act intended as a unified coverage of its subject matter, no part of it is to be construed as impliedly repealed by subsequent legislation if that construction can reasonably be avoided.

§ 1.105. [Administration of Remedies; Enforcement]

(a) The remedies provided by this Act shall be so administered that an aggrieved party may recover appropriate damages. The aggrieved party has a duty to mitigate damages.

(b) Any right or obligation declared by this Act is enforceable by action unless the provision declaring it specifies a different and limited effect.

§ 1.106. [Settlement of Disputed Claim or Right]

A claim or right arising under this Act or on a rental agreement, if disputed in good faith, may be settled by agreement.

PART II. SCOPE AND JURISDICTION

§ 1.201. [Territorial Application]

This Act applies to, regulates, and determines rights, obligations, and remedies under a rental agreement, wherever made, for a dwelling unit located within this state.

§ 1.202. [Exclusions from Application of Act]

Unless created to avoid the application of this Act, the following arrangements are not governed by this Act:

(1) residence at an institution, public or private, if incidental to detention or the provision of medical, geriatric, educational, counseling, religious, or similar service;

(2) occupancy under a contract of sale of a dwelling unit or the property of which it is a part, if the occupant is the purchaser or a person who succeeds to his interest;

(3) occupancy by a member of a fraternal or social organization in the portion of a structure operated for the benefit of the organization;

(4) transient occupancy in a hotel, or motel [or lodgings [subject to cite state transient lodgings or room occupancy excise tax act]];

(5) occupancy by an employee of a landlord whose right to occupancy is conditional upon employment in and about the premises;

(6) occupancy by an owner of a condominium unit or a holder of a proprietary lease in a cooperative;

(7) occupancy under a rental agreement covering premises used by the occupant primarily for agricultural purposes.

§ 1.203. [Jurisdiction and Service of Process]

(a) The _____ court of this state may exercise jurisdiction over any landlord with respect to any conduct in this state governed by this Act or with respect to any claim arising from a transaction subject to this Act. In addition to any other method provided by rule or by statute, personal jurisdiction over a landlord may be acquired in a civil action or proceeding instituted in the court by the service of process in the manner provided by this section.

(b) If a landlord is not a resident of this state or is a corporation not authorized to do business in this state and engages in any conduct in this state governed by this Act, or engages in a transaction subject to this Act, he may designate an agent upon whom service of process may be made in this state. The agent shall be a resident of this state or a corporation authorized to do business in this state. The designation shall be in writing and filed with the [Secretary of State]. If no designation is made and filed or if process cannot be served in this state upon the designated agent, process may be served upon the [Secretary of State], but service upon him is not effective unless the plaintiff or petitioner forthwith mails a copy of the process and pleading by registered or certified mail to the defendant or respondent at his last reasonably ascertainable address. An affidavit of compliance with this section shall be filed with the clerk of the court on or before the return day of the process, if any, or within any further time the court allows.]

PART III. GENERAL DEFINITIONS AND PRINCIPLES OF INTERPRETATION: NOTICE

§ 1.301. [General Definitions]

Subject to additional definitions contained in subsequent Articles of this Act which apply to specific Articles or Parts thereof, and unless the context otherwise requires, in this Act

(1) "action" includes recoupment, counterclaim, set-off, suit in equity, and any other proceeding in which rights are determined, including an action for possession;

(2) "building and housing codes" include any law, ordinance, or governmental regulation concerning fitness for habitation, or the construction, maintenance, operation, occupancy, use, or appearance of any premises, or dwelling unit;

(3) "dwelling unit" means a structure or the part of a structure that is used as a home, residence, or sleeping place by one person who maintains a household or by 2 or more persons who maintain a common household;

(4) "good faith" means honesty in fact in the conduct of the transaction concerned;

(5) "landlord" means the owner, lessor, or sublessor of the dwelling unit or the building of which it is a part, and it also means a manager of the premises who fails to disclose as required by Section 2.102;

(6) "organization" includes a corporation, government, governmental subdivision or agency, business trust, estate, trust, partnership or association, 2 or more persons having a joint or common interest, and any other legal or commercial entity;

(7) "owner" means one or more persons, jointly or severally, in whom is vested (i) all or part of the legal title to property or (ii) all or part of the beneficial ownership and a right to present use and enjoyment of the premises. The term includes a mortgagee in possession;

(8) "person" includes an individual or organization;

(9) "premises" means a dwelling unit and the structure of which it is a part and facilities and appurtenances therein and grounds, areas, and facilities held out for the use of tenants generally or whose use is promised to the tenant;

(10) "rent" means all payments to be made to or for the benefit of the landlord under the rental agreement;

(11) "rental agreement" means all agreements, written or oral, and valid rules and regulations adopted under Section 3.102 embodying the terms and conditions concerning the use and occupancy of a dwelling unit and premises;

(12) "roomer" means a person occupying a dwelling unit that does not include a toilet and either a bath tub or a shower and a refrigerator, stove, and kitchen sink, all provided by the landlord, and where one or more of these facilities are used in common by occupants in the structure;

(13) "single family residence" means a structure maintained and used as a single dwelling unit. Notwithstanding that a dwelling unit shares one or more walls with another dwelling unit, it is a single family residence if it has direct access to a street or thoroughfare and shares neither heating facilities, hot water equipment, nor any other essential facility or service with any other dwelling unit;

(14) "tenant" means a person entitled under a rental agreement to occupy a dwelling unit to the exclusion of others.

§ 1.302. [Obligation of Good Faith]

Every duty under this Act and every act which must be performed as a condition precedent to the exercise of a right or remedy under this Act imposes an obligation of good faith in its performance or enforcement.

§ 1.303. [Unconscionability]

(a) If the court, as a matter of law, finds

(1) a rental agreement or any provision thereof was unconscionable when made, the court may refuse to enforce the agreement, enforce the remainder of the agreement without the unconscionable provision, or limit the application of any unconscionable provision to avoid an unconscionable result; or

(2) a settlement in which a party waives or agrees to forego a claim or right under this Act or under a rental agreement was unconscionable when made, the court may refuse to enforce the settlement, enforce the remainder of the settlement without the unconscionable provision, or limit the application of any unconscionable provision to avoid an unconscionable result.

(b) If unconscionability is put into issue by a party or by the court upon its own motion the parties shall be afforded a reasonable opportunity to present evidence as to the setting, purpose, and effect of the rental agreement or settlement to aid the court in making the determination.

§ 1.304. [Notice]

(a) A person has notice of a fact if

(1) he has actual knowledge of it,

(2) he has received a notice or notification of it, or

(3) from all the facts and circumstances known to him at the time in question he has reason to know that it exists.

A person "knows" or "has knowledge" of a fact if he has actual knowledge of it.

(b) A person "notifies" or "gives" a notice or notification to another person by taking steps reasonably calculated to inform the other in ordinary course whether or not the other actually comes to know of it. A person "receives" a notice or notification when

(1) it comes to his attention; or

(2) in the case of the landlord, it is delivered at the place of business of the landlord through which the rental agreement was made or at any place held out by him as the place for receipt of the communication; or

(3) in the case of the tenant, it is delivered in hand to the tenant or mailed by registered or certified mail to him at the place held out by him as the place for receipt of the communication, or in the absence of such designation, to his last known place of residence.

(c) "Notice," knowledge of a notice or notification received by an organization is effective for a particular transaction from the time it is brought to the attention of the individual conducting that transaction, and in any event from the time it would have been brought to his attention if the organization had exercised reasonable diligence.

PART IV. GENERAL PROVISIONS

§ 1.401. [Terms and Conditions of Rental Agreement]

(a) A landlord and a tenant may include in a rental agreement terms and conditions not prohibited by this Act or other rule of law, including rent, term of the agreement, and other provisions governing the rights and obligations of the parties.

(b) In absence of agreement, the tenant shall pay as rent the fair rental value for the use and occupancy of the dwelling unit.

(c) Rent is payable without demand or notice at the time and place agreed upon by the parties. Unless otherwise agreed, rent is payable at the dwelling unit and periodic rent is payable at the beginning of any term of one month or less and otherwise in equal monthly installments at the beginning of each month. Unless otherwise agreed, rent is uniformly apportionable from day-to-day.

(d) Unless the rental agreement fixes a definite term, the tenancy is week-to-week in case of a roomer who pays weekly rent, and in all other cases month-to-month.

§ 1.402. [Effect of Unsigned or Undelivered Rental Agreement]

(a) If the landlord does not sign and deliver a written rental agreement signed and delivered to him by the tenant, acceptance of rent without reservation by the landlord gives the rental agreement the same effect as if it had been signed and delivered by the landlord.

(b) If the tenant does not sign and deliver a written rental agreement signed and delivered to him by the landlord, acceptance of possession and payment of rent without reservation gives the rental agreement the same effect as if it had been signed and delivered by the tenant.

(c) If a rental agreement given effect by the operation of this section provides for a term longer than one year, it is effective for only one year.

§ 1.403. [Prohibited Provisions in Rental Agreements]

(a) A rental agreement may not provide that the tenant:

(1) agrees to waive or forego rights or remedies under this Act;

(2) authorizes any person to confess judgment on a claim arising out of the rental agreement;

(3) agrees to pay the landlord's attorney's fees; or

(4) agrees to the exculpation or limitation of any liability of the landlord arising under law or to indemnify the landlord for that liability or the costs connected therewith.

(b) A provision prohibited by subsection (a) included in a rental agreement is unenforceable. If a landlord deliberately uses a rental agreement containing provisions known by him to be prohibited, the tenant may recover in addition to his actual damages an amount up to [3] months' periodic rent and reasonable attorney's fees.

§ 1.404. [Separation of Rents and Obligations to Maintain Property Forbidden]

A rental agreement, assignment, conveyance, trust deed, or security instrument may not permit the receipt of rent free of the obligation to comply with Section 2.104(a).

ARTICLE II: LANDLORD OBLIGATIONS

§ 2.101. [Security Deposits; Prepaid Rent]

(a) A landlord may not demand or receive security, however denominated, in an amount or value in excess of [1] month[s] periodic rent.

(b) Upon termination of the tenancy property or money held by the landlord as security may be applied to the payment of accrued rent and the amount of damages which the landlord has suffered by reason of the tenant's noncompliance with Section 3.101 all as itemized by the landlord in a written notice delivered to the tenant together with the amount due [14] days after termination of the tenancy and delivery of possession and demand by the tenant.

(c) If the landlord fails to comply with subsection (b) or if he fails to return any prepaid rent required to be paid to the tenants under this Act the tenant may recover the property and money due him together with damages in an amount equal to [twice] the amount wrongfully withheld and reasonable attorney's fees.

(d) This section does not preclude the landlord or tenant from recovering other damages to which he may be entitled under this Act.

(e) The holder of the landlord's interest in the premises at the time of the termination of the tenancy is bound by this section.

§ 2.102. [Disclosure]

(a) A landlord or any person authorized to enter into a rental agreement on his behalf shall disclose to the tenant in writing at or before the commencement of the tenancy the name and address of

(1) the person authorized to manage the premises; and

(2) an owner of the premises or a person authorized to act for and on behalf of the owner for the purpose of service of process and receiving and receipting for notices and demands.

(b) The information required to be furnished by this section shall be kept current and this section extends to and is enforceable against any successor landlord, owner, or manager.

(c) A person who fails to comply with subsection (a) becomes an agent of each person who is a landlord for:

(1) service of process and receiving and receipting for notices and demands; and

(2) performing the obligations of the landlord under this Act and under the rental agreement and expending or making available for the purpose all rent collected from the premises.

§ 2.103. [Landlord to Deliver Possession of Dwelling Unit]

At the commencement of the term a landlord shall deliver possession of the premises to the tenant in compliance with the rental agreement and Section 2.104. The landlord may bring an action for possession against any person wrongfully in possession and may recover the damages provided in Section 4.301(c).

§ 2.104. [Landlord to Maintain Premises]

(a) A landlord shall

(1) comply with the requirements of applicable building and housing codes materially affecting health and safety;

(2) make all repairs and do whatever is necessary to put and keep the premises in a fit and habitable condition;

(3) keep all common areas of the premises in a clean and safe condition;

(4) maintain in good and safe working order and condition all electrical, plumbing, sanitary, heating, ventilating, air-conditioning, and other facilities and appliances, including elevators, supplied or required to be supplied by him;

(5) provide and maintain appropriate receptacles and conveniences for the removal of ashes, garbage, rubbish, and other waste incidental to the occupancy of the dwelling unit and arrange for their removal; and

(6) supply running water and reasonable amounts of hot water at all times and reasonable heat [between [October 1] and [May 1]] except where the building that includes the dwelling unit is not required by law to be equipped for that purpose, or the dwelling unit is so constructed that heat or hot water is generated by an installation within the exclusive control of the tenant and supplied by a direct public utility connection.

(b) If the duty imposed by paragraph (1) of subsection (a) is greater than any duty imposed by any other paragraph of that subsection, the landlord's duty shall be determined by reference to paragraph (1) of subsection (a).

(c) The landlord and tenant of a single family residence may agree in writing that the tenant perform the landlord's duties specified in paragraphs (5) and (6) of subsection (a) and also specified repairs, maintenance tasks, alterations, and remodeling, but only if the transaction is entered into in good faith.

(d) The landlord and tenant of any dwelling unit other than a single family residence may agree that the tenant is to perform specified repairs, maintenance tasks, alterations, or remodeling only if

(1) the agreement of the parties is entered into in good faith and is set forth in a separate writing signed by the parties and supported by adequate consideration;

(2) the work is not necessary to cure noncompliance with subsection (a)(1) of this section; and

(3) the agreement does not diminish or affect the obligation of the landlord to other tenants in the premises.

(e) The landlord may not treat performance of the separate agreement described in subsection (d) as a condition to any obligation or performance of any rental agreement.

§ 2.105. [Limitation of Liability]

(a) Unless otherwise agreed, a landlord who conveys premises that include a dwelling unit subject to a rental agreement in a good faith sale to a bona fide purchaser is relieved of liability under the rental agreement and this Act as to events occurring after written notice to the tenant of the conveyance. However, he remains liable to the tenant for all security recoverable by the tenant under Section 2.101 and all prepaid rent.

(b) Unless otherwise agreed, a manager of premises that include a dwelling unit is relieved of liability under the rental agreement and this Act as to events occurring after written notice to the tenant of the termination of his management.

ARTICLE III: TENANT OBLIGATIONS

§ 3.101. [Tenant to Maintain Dwelling Unit]

A tenant shall

(1) comply with all obligations primarily imposed upon tenants by applicable provisions of building and housing codes materially affecting health and safety;

(2) keep that part of the premises that he occupies and uses as clean and safe as the condition of the premises permit;

(3) dispose from his dwelling unit all ashes, garbage, rubbish, and other waste in a clean and safe manner;

(4) keep all plumbing fixtures in the dwelling unit or used by the tenant as clear as their condition permits;

(5) use in a reasonable manner all electrical, plumbing, sanitary, heating, ventilating, air-conditioning, and other facilities and appliances including elevators in the premises;

(6) not deliberately or negligently destroy, deface, damage, impair, or remove any part of the premises or knowingly permit any person to do so; and

(7) conduct himself and require other persons on the premises with his consent to conduct themselves in a manner that will not disturb his neighbors' peaceful enjoyment of the premises.

§ 3.102. [Rules and Regulations]

(a) A landlord, from time to time, may adopt a rule or regulation, however described, concerning the tenant's use and occupancy of the premises. It is enforceable against the tenant only if

(1) its purpose is to promote the convenience, safety, or welfare of the tenants in the premises, preserve the landlord's property from abusive use, or make a fair distribution of services and facilities held out for the tenants generally;

(2) it is reasonably related to the purpose of which it is adopted;

(3) it applies to all tenants in the premises in a fair manner;

(4) it is sufficiently explicit in its prohibition, direction, or limitation of the tenant's conduct to fairly inform him of what he must or must not do to comply;

(5) it is not for the purpose of evading the obligations of the landlord; and

(6) the tenant has notice of it at the time he enters into the rental agreement, or when it is adopted.

(b) If a rule or regulation is adopted after the tenant enters into the rental agreement that works a substantial modification of his bargain it is not valid unless the tenant consents to it in writing.

§ 3.103. [Access]

(a) A tenant shall not unreasonably withhold consent to the landlord to enter into the dwelling unit in order to inspect the premises, make necessary or agreed repairs, decorations, alterations, or improvements, supply necessary or agreed services, or exhibit the dwelling unit to prospective or actual purchasers, mortgagees, tenants, workmen, or contractors.

(b) A landlord may enter the dwelling unit without consent of the tenant in case of emergency.

(c) A landlord shall not abuse the right of access or use it to harass the tenant. Except in case of emergency or unless it is impracticable to do so, the landlord shall give the tenant at least [2] days' notice of his intent to enter and may enter only at reasonable times.

(d) A landlord has no other right of access except [list exceptions].

§ 3.104. [Tenant to Use and Occupy]

Unless otherwise agreed, a tenant shall occupy his dwelling unit only as a dwelling unit. The rental agreement may require that the tenant notify the landlord of any anticipated extended absence from the premises [in excess of [7] days] no later than the first day of the extended absence.

ARTICLE IV: REMEDIES

PART I. TENANT REMEDIES

§ 4.101. [Noncompliance by the Landlord - In General]

(a) Except as provided in this Act, if there is a material noncompliance by the landlord with the rental agreement or a noncompliance with Section 2.104 materially affecting health and safety, the tenant may deliver a written notice to the landlord specifying the acts and omissions constituting the breach and that the rental agreement will terminate upon a date not less than [30] days after receipt of the notice if the breach is not remedied in [14] days, and the rental agreement shall terminate as provided in the notice subject to the following:

> (1) If the breach is remedial by repairs, the payment of damages or otherwise and the landlord adequately remedies the breach before the date specified in the notice, the rental agreement shall not terminate by reason of the breach.

> (2) If substantially the same act or omission which constituted a prior noncompliance of which notice was given recurs within [6] months, the tenant may terminate the rental agreement upon at least [14 days'] written notice specifying the breach and the date of termination of the rental agreement.

> (3) The tenant may not terminate for a condition caused by the deliberate or negligent act or omission of the tenant, a member of his family, or other person on the premises with his consent.

(b) Except as provided in this Act, the tenant may recover actual damages and obtain injunctive relief for noncompliance by the landlord with the rental agreement or Section 2.104. If the landlord's noncompliance is willful the tenant may recover reasonable attorney's fees.

(c) The remedy provided in subsection (b) is in addition to any right of the tenant arising under Section 4.101(a).

(d) If the rental agreement is terminated, the landlord shall return all security recoverable by the tenant under Section 2.101 and all prepaid rent.

§ 4.102. [Failure to Deliver Possession]

(a) If the landlord fails to deliver possession of the dwelling unit to the tenant as provided in Section 2.103, rent abates until possession is delivered and the tenant may

(1) terminate the rental agreement upon at least [5] days' written notice to the landlord and upon termination the landlord shall return all prepaid rent and security; or

(2) demand performance of the rental agreement by the landlord and, if the tenant elects, obtain posession of the dwelling unit from the landlord or any person wrongfully in possession and recover the actual damages sustained by him.

(b) If a person's failure to deliver possession is willful and not in good faith, an aggrieved person may recover from that person an amount not more than [3] months' periodic rent or [threefold] the actual damages sustained, whichever is greater, and reasonable attorney's fees.

§ 4.103. [Self-Help for Minor Defects]

(a) If the landlord fails to comply with the rental agreement or Section 2.104, and the reasonable cost of compliance is less than [$100], or an amount equal to [one-half] the periodic rent, whichever amount is greater, the tenant may recover damages for the breach under Section 4.101(b) or may notify the landlord of his intention to correct the condition at the landlord's expense. If the landlord fails to comply within [14] days after being notified by the tenant in writing or as promptly as conditions require in case of emergency, the tenant may cause the work to be done in a workmanlike manner and, after submitting to the landlord an itemized statement, deduct from his rent the actual and reasonable cost or the fair and reasonable value of the work, not exceeding the amount specified in this subsection.

(b) A tenant may not repair at the landlord's expense if the condition was caused by the deliberate or negligent act or omission of the tenant, a member of his family, or other person on the premises with his consent.

§ 4.104. [Wrongful Failure to Supply Heat, Water, Hot Water, or Essential Services]

(a) If contrary to the rental agreement or Section 2.104 the landlord willfully or negligently fails to supply heat, running water, hot water, electric, gas, or other essential service, the tenant may give written notice to the landlord specifying the breach and may

(1) take reasonable and appropriate measures to secure reasonable amounts of heat, hot water, running water, electric, gas, and other

essential service during the period of the landlord's noncompliance and deduct their actual and reasonable cost from the rent; or

(2) recover damages based upon the diminution in the fair rental value of the dwelling unit; or

(3) procure reasonable substitute housing during the period of the landlord's noncompliance, in which case the tenant is excused from paying rent for the period of the landlord's noncompliance.

(b) In addition to the remedy provided in paragraph (3) of subsection (a) the tenant may recover the actual and reasonable cost or fair and reasonable value of the substitute housing not in excess of an amount equal to the periodic rent, and in any case under subsection (a) reasonable attorney's fees.

(c) If the tenant proceeds under this section, he may not proceed under Section 4.101 or Section 4.103 as to that breach.

(d) Rights of the tenant under this section do not arise until he has given notice to the landlord or if the condition was caused by the deliberate or negligent act or omission of the tenant, a member of his family, or other person on the premises with his consent.

§ 4.105. [Landlord's Noncompliance as Defense to Action for Possession or Rent]

(a) In an action for possession based upon nonpayment of the rent or in an action for rent when the tenant is in possession, the tenant may [counterclaim] for any amount he may recover under the rental agreement or this Act. In that event the court from time to time may order the tenant to pay into court all or part of the rent accrued and thereafter accruing, and shall determine the amount due to each party. The party to whom a net amount is owed shall be paid first from the money paid into court, and the balance by the other party. If no rent remains due after application of this section, judgment shall be entered for the tenant in the action for possession. If the defense or counterclaim by the tenant is without merit and is not raised in good faith, the landlord may recover reasonable attorney's fees.

(b) In an action for rent when the tenant is not in possession, he may [counterclaim] as provided in subsection (a) but is not required to pay any rent into court.

§ 4.106. [Fire or Casualty Damage]

(a) If the dwelling unit or premises are damaged or destroyed by fire or casualty to an extent that enjoyment of the dwelling unit is substantially impaired, the tenant may

(1) immediately vacate the premises and notify the landlord in writing within [14] days thereafter of his intention to terminate the rental agreement, in which case the rental agreement terminates as of the date of vacating; or

(2) if continued occupancy is lawful, vacate any part of the dwelling unit rendered unusable by the fire or casualty, in which case the tenant's liability for rent is reduced in proportion to the diminution in the fair rental value of the dwelling unit.

(b) If the rental agreement is terminated the landlord shall return all security recoverable under Section 2.101 and all prepaid rent. Accounting for rent in the event of termination or apportionment shall be made as of the date of the fire or casualty.

§ 4.107. [Tenant's Remedies for Landlord's Unlawful Ouster, Exclusion, or Diminution of Service]

If a landlord unlawfully removes or excludes the tenant from the premises or willfully diminishes services to the tenant by interrupting or causing the interruption of heat, running water, hot water, electric, gas, or other essential service, the tenant may recover possession or terminate the rental agreement and, in either case, recover an amount not more than [3] months' periodic rent or [threefold] the actual damages sustained by him, whichever is greater, and reasonable attorney's fees. If the rental agreement is terminated the landlord shall return all security recoverable under Section 2.101 and all prepaid rent.

PART II. LANDLORD REMEDIES

§ 4.201. [Noncompliance with Rental Agreement; Failure to Pay Rent]

(a) Except as provided in this Act, if there is a material noncompliance by the tenant with the rental agreement or a noncompliance with Section 3.101 materially affecting health and safety, the landlord may deliver a written notice to the tenant specifying the acts and omissions constituting the breach and that the rental agreement will terminate upon a date not less than [30] days after receipt of the notice. If the breach is not remedied in [14] days, the rental agreement shall terminate as provided in the notice subject to the following. If the breach is remediable by repairs or the payment of damages or otherwise and the tenant adequately remedies the breach before the date specified in the notice, the rental agreement shall not terminate. If substantially the same act or omission which constituted a prior noncompliance of which notice was given recurs within [6] months, the landlord may terminate the rental agreement upon at least [14] days' written notice specifying the breach and the date of termination of the rental agreement.

(b) If rent is unpaid when due and the tenant fails to pay rent within [14] days after written notice by the landlord of nonpayment and his intention to terminate the rental agreement if the rent is not paid within that period, the landlord may terminate the rental agreement.

(c) Except as provided in this Act, the landlord may recover actual damages and obtain injunctive relief for noncompliance by the tenant with the rental agreement or Section 3.101. If the tenant's noncompliance is willful the landlord may recover reasonable attorney's fees.

§ 4.202. [Failure to Maintain]

If there is noncompliance by the tenant with Section 3.101 materially affecting health and safety that can be remedied by repair, replacement of a damaged item, or cleaning, and the tenant fails to comply as promptly as conditions require in case of emergency or within [14] days after written notice by the landlord specifying the breach and requesting that the tenant remedy it within that period of time, the landlord may enter the dwelling unit and cause the work to be done in a workmanlike manner and submit the itemized bill for the actual and reasonable cost or the fair and reasonable value thereof as rent on the next date periodic rent is due, or if the rental agreement has terminated, for immediate payment.

§ 4.203. [Remedies for Absence, Nonuse and Abandonment]

(a) If the rental agreement requires the tenant to give notice to the landlord of an anticipated extended absence [in excess of [7] days] pursuant to Section 3.104 and the tenant willfully fails to do so, the landlord may recover actual damages from the tenant.

(b) During any absence of the tenant in excess of [7] days, the landlord may enter the dwelling unit at times reasonably necessary.

(c) If the tenant abandons the dwelling unit, the landlord shall make reasonable efforts to rent it at a fair rental. If the landlord rents the dwelling unit for a term beginning before the expiration of the rental agreement, it terminates as of the date of the new tenancy. If the landlord fails to use reasonable efforts to rent the dwelling unit at a fair rental or if the landlord accepts the abandonment as a surrender, the rental agreement is deemed to be terminated by the landlord as of the date the landlord has notice of the abandonment. If the tenancy is from month-to-month or week-to-week, the term of the rental agreement for this purpose is deemed to be a month or a week, as the case may be.

§ 4.204. [Waiver of Landlord's Right to Terminate]

Acceptance of rent with knowledge of a default by the tenant or acceptance of performance by him that varies from the terms of the rental agreement constitutes a waiver of the landlord's right to terminate the rental agreement for that breach, unless otherwise agreed after the breach has occurred.

§ 4.205. [Landlord Liens; Distress for Rent]

(a) A lien or security interest on behalf of the landlord in the tenant's household goods is not enforceable unless perfected before the effective date of this Act.

(b) Distraint for rent is abolished.

§ 4.206. [Remedy after Termination]

If the rental agreement is terminated, the landlord has a claim for possession and for rent and a separate claim for actual damages for breach of the rental agreement and reasonable attorney's fees as provided in Section 4.201(c).

§ 4.207. [Recovery of Possession Limited]

A landlord may not recover or take possession of the dwelling unit by action or otherwise, including willful diminution of services to the tenant by interrupting or causing the interruption of heat, running water, hot water, electric, gas, or other essential service to the tenant, except in case of abandonment, surrender, or as permitted in this Act.

PART III. PERIODIC TENANCY; HOLDOVER; ABUSE OF ACCESS

§ 4.301. [Periodic Tenancy; Holdover Remedies]

(a) The landlord or the tenant may terminate a week-to-week tenancy by a written notice given to the other at least [10] days before the termination date specified in the notice.

(b) The landlord or the tenant may terminate a month-to-month tenancy by a written notice given to the other at least [60] days before the periodic rental date specified in the notice.

(c) If the tenant remains in possession without the landlord's consent after expiration of the term of the rental agreement or its termination, the landlord may bring an action for possession and if the tenant's holdover is willful and not in good faith the landlord may also recover an amount not more than [3] month's periodic rent or [threefold] the actual damages sustained by him, whichever is greater, and reasonable attorney's fees. If the landlord consents to the tenant's continued occupancy, Section 1.401(d) applies.

§ 4.302. [Landlord and Tenant Remedies for Abuse of Access]

(a) If the tenant refuses to allow lawful access, the landlord may obtain injunctive relief to compel access, or terminate the rental agreement. In either case the landlord may recover actual damages and reasonable attorney's fees.

(b) If the landlord makes an unlawful entry or a lawful entry in an unreasonable manner or makes repeated demands for entry otherwise lawful but which have the effect of unreasonably harassing the tenant, the tenant may obtain injunctive relief to prevent the recurrence of the conduct or terminate the rental agreement. In either case the tenant may recover actual damages [not less than an amount equal to [1] month's rent] and reasonable attorney's fees.

ARTICLE V: RETALIATORY CONDUCT

§ 5.101. [Retaliatory Conduct Prohibited]

(a) Except as provided in this section, a landlord may not retaliate by increasing rent or decreasing services or by bringing or threatening to bring an action for possession after:

(1) the tenant has complained to a governmental agency charged with responsibility for enforcement of a building or housing code of a violation applicable to the premises materially affecting health and safety; or

(2) the tenant has complained to the landlord of a violation under Section 2.104; or

(3) the tenant has organized or become a member of a tenant's union or similar organization.

(b) If the landlord acts in violation of subsection (a), the tenant is entitled to the remedies provided in Section 4.107 and has a defense in any retaliatory action against him for possession. In an action by or against the tenant, evidence of a complaint within [1] year before the alleged act of retaliation creates a presumption that the landlord's conduct was in retaliation. The presumption does not arise if the tenant made the complaint after notice of a proposed rent increase or diminution of services. "Presumption" means that the trier of fact must find the existence of the fact presumed unless and until evidence is introduced which would support a finding of its nonexistence.

(c) Notwithstanding subsections (a) and (b), a landlord may bring an action for possession if:

(1) the violation of the applicable building or housing code was caused primarily by lack of reasonable care by the tenant, a member of his family, or other person on the premises with his consent; or

(2) the tenant is in default in rent; or

(3) compliance with the applicable building or housing code requires alteration, remodeling, or demolition which would effectively deprive the tenant of use of the dwelling unit.

(d) The maintenance of an action under subsection (c) does not release the landlord from liability under Section 4.101(b).

ARTICLE VI: EFFECTIVE DATE AND REPEALER

§ 6.101. [Effective Date]

This Act shall become effective on _____. It applies to rental agreements entered into or extended or renewed on and after that date.

§ 6.102. [Specific Repealer]

The following Acts and parts of Acts are hereby repealed: [List appropriate Acts]

§ 6.103. [Savings Clause]

Transactions entered into before the effective date of this Act, and not extended or renewed on and after that date, and the rights, duties, and interests flowing from them remain valid and may be terminated, completed, consummated, or enforced as required or permitted by any statute or other law amended or repealed by this Act as though the repeal or amendment had not occurred.

§ 6.104. [Severability]

If any provision of this Act or the application thereof to any person or circumstance is held invalid, the invalidity does not affect other provisions or application of this Act which can be given effect without the invalid provision or application, and to this end the provisions of this Act are severable.

GLOSSARY

Abandonment—The tenant's remedy of moving out of a rental unit that is uninhabitable and that the landlord has not repaired within a reasonable time after receiving notice of the defects from the tenant.

Act of God—Manifestation of the forces of nature which are unpredictable and difficult to anticipate, such as lightning and earthquakes.

Agent—One who represents another known as the principal.

Anticipatory Breach of Contract—A breach committed before the arrival of the actual time of required performance.

Appeal—A request to a higher court to review a lower court's decision in a lawsuit.

Arbitration—Using a neutral third person to resolve a dispute instead of going to court. Unless the parties have agreed otherwise, the parties must follow the arbitrator's decision.

Arbitrator—A neutral third person, agreed to by the parties to a dispute, who hears and decides the dispute. An arbitrator is not a judge, but the parties must follow the arbitrator's decision. The decision is said to be "binding" on the parties.

Arrears—Payments which are due but not yet paid.

Assignee—An assignee is a person to whom an assignment is made, also known as a grantee.

Assignment—An agreement between the original tenant and a new tenant by which the new tenant takes over the lease of a rental unit and becomes responsible to the landlord for everything that was required by the original tenant. The original tenant is still responsible to the landlord if the new tenant doesn't live up to the lease obligations.

Boilerplate—Refers to standard language found almost universally in certain documents.

Breach of Contract—The failure, without any legal excuse, to perform any promise which forms the whole or the part of a contract.

Breach of Duty—In a general sense, any violation or omission of a legal or moral duty.

Breach of Warranty—An infraction of an express or implied agreement as to the title, quality, content or condition of a thing which is sold.

Cease and Desist Order—A court order prohibiting an unlawful course of conduct or activity.

Certificate of Occupancy—A document issued by local governmental authorities which certifies that a building conforms to local building code regulations.

Chattel—Any tangible, movable piece of personal property as opposed to real property.

Commission—Compensation for services performed which is based on a percentage of an agreed amount.

Common Area—In landlord-tenant law, refers to the area of the premises which is used by all tenants, e.g., hallways, elevators, etc.

Condominium—The individual ownership of a single unit in a multi-unit structure together with an interest in the common areas.

Consideration—Something of value exchanged between parties to a contract, which is a requirement of a valid contract.

Contract—A contract is an agreement between two or more persons which creates an obligation to do or not to do a particular thing.

Cooperative—Ownership of stock in a corporation which owns property that is subdivided into individual units.

Covenant—A covenant is an agreement or promise to do or not to do a particular thing, as to bind oneself in contract.

Credit Report—A credit report refers to the document from a credit reporting agency setting forth a credit rating and pertinent financial data concerning a person or a company, which is used in evaluating the applicant's financial stability. A credit report shows, for example, whether the person pays his or her bills on time, has delinquent or charged-off accounts, has been sued, and is subject to court judgments.

Credit Reporting Agency—A business that keeps records of people's credit histories, and that reports credit history information to prospective creditors, including landlords.

Default—Default is a failure to discharge a duty or do that which ought to be done.

Default Judgment—A judgment issued by the court, without a hearing, after the tenant has failed to file a response to the landlord's complaint.

Demurrer—A legal response that a tenant can file in an unlawful detainer lawsuit to test the legal sufficiency of the charges made in the landlord's complaint.

Discrimination in Rental Housing—As it relates to rental housing, discrimination occurs when a person is denied housing, is told that housing is not available when the housing is actually available at that time, providing housing under inferior terms, or is provided segregated housing, because of a person's race, color, national origin, ancestry, religion, sex, sexual preference, age, disability, whether the person is married, or whether there are children under the age of 18 in the person's household. Discrimination also can occur upon the refusal to make reasonable accommodation for a person with a disability.

Domicile—The one place designated as an individual's permanent home.

Duty—The obligation, to which the law will give recognition and effect, to conform to a particular standard of conduct toward another.

Escrow—The arrangement for holding instruments or money which is not to be released until certain specified conditions are met.

Escrow Account—A bank account into which a tenant deposits withheld rent, to be withdrawn only when the landlord has corrected uninhabitable conditions in the rental unit or when the tenant is ordered by a court to pay withheld rent to the landlord.

Eviction—A court-administered proceeding for removing a tenant from a rental unit because the tenant has violated the rental agreement or did not comply with a notice ending the tenancy, also called an "unlawful detainer" lawsuit.

Eviction Notice—A notice that the landlord serves on the tenant when the tenant has violated the lease or rental agreement, also known as "three-day notice." The three-day notice usually instructs the tenant to either leave the rental unit or comply with the lease or rental agreement, for example, by paying past-due rent, within the three-day period.

Excuse—A matter alleged to be a reason for relief or exemption from some duty or obligation.

Fair Housing Organizations—Organizations that help renters resolve housing discrimination problems.

Federal Stay—An order of a federal bankruptcy court that temporarily stops proceedings in a state court, including an eviction proceeding.

Fixture—Chattel which has become permanently and physically attached to real property, and which would not be easily removed.

Forcible Entry—The entry on real property, against the possessor's will, without legal authority.

Freehold Estate—A real property estate with no measurable length of time or termination date.

Grace Period—In contract law, a period specified in a contract which is beyond the due date but during which time payment will be accepted without penalty.

Guest—A person who does not have the rights of a tenant, such as a person who stays in a transient hotel for fewer than seven days.

Habitable—A rental unit in which the conditions are safe, healthy and fit for occupancy, and that substantially complies with those building and safety code standards that materially affect tenants' health and safety is said to be "habitable."

Hostile Possession—The actual possession of real property without the permission of the legal owner, with a claim of implied ownership by the possessor.

Holding Deposit—A deposit that a tenant gives to a landlord to hold a rental unit until the tenant pays the first month's rent and the security deposit.

Implied Warranty of Habitability—A legal rule that requires landlords to maintain their rental units in a condition fit for human beings to live in. In addition, a rental unit must substantially comply with building and housing code standards that materially affect tenants' health and safety.

Impossibility—Impossibility is a defense to breach of contract and arises when performance is impossible due to the destruction of the subject matter of the contract or the death of a person necessary for performance.

Improvement—The development of land or structures to increase the property value.

Invitee—One who enters another's property by invitation.

Item of Information—Information in a credit report that causes a creditor to deny credit or take other adverse action against an applicant, such as refusing to rent a rental unit to the applicant.

Joint and Several—The rights and liabilities shared among a group of people individually and collectively.

Landlord—A business or person who owns a rental unit, and who rents or leases the rental unit to another person, called a tenant.

Lease—A rental agreement, usually in writing, that establishes all the terms of the agreement and that lasts for a predetermined length of time, e.g., six months or one year.

Legal Aid Organizations—Organizations that provide free legal advice, representation, and other legal services in noncriminal cases to economically disadvantaged persons.

Liability—Liability refers to one's obligation to do or refrain from doing something, such as the payment of a debt.

Lockout—When a landlord locks a tenant out of the rental unit with the intent of terminating the tenancy. Lockouts, and all other self-help eviction remedies, are illegal.

Lodger—A person who lives in a room in a house where the owner lives. The owner can enter all areas occupied by the lodger, and has overall control of the house.

Mediation—A process in which a neutral third person meets with the parties to a dispute in order to assist them in formulating a voluntary solution to the dispute.

Mitigation of Damages—The requirement that a person damaged due to another's acts, such as a breach of contract, must act reasonably to avoid or limit their losses, or risk denial of recovery for damages which could have been avoided.

Motion to Quash Service of Summons—A legal response that a tenant can file in an unlawful detainer lawsuit if the tenant believes that the landlord did not properly serve the summons and complaint.

Negligence—A person's carelessness—i.e., failure to use ordinary or reasonable care—that results in injury to another person or damage to another person's property.

Nonfreehold Estate—A leasehold.

Novation—In an assignment situation, a novation is an agreement by the landlord, the original tenant, and the new tenant that makes the new tenant, rather than the original tenant, solely responsible to the landlord.

Nuisance—The disturbance of another's use of their property, rendering continued use uncomfortable or inconvenient.

Periodic Rental Agreement—An oral or written rental agreement that states the length of time between rent payments, e.g., a week or a month, but not the total number of weeks or months that the agreement will be in effect.

Prepaid Rental Listing Services—Businesses that sell lists of available rental units.

Privity of Contract—Privity of contract refers to the relationship between the parties to a contract.

Quiet Enjoyment—The right of an owner or lessor to have unimpaired use and enjoyment out of the property.

Reformation—An equitable remedy which calls for the rewriting of a contract involving a mutual mistake or fraud.

Relief from Forfeiture—An order by a court in an unlawful detainer—i.e., eviction—lawsuit that allows the losing tenant to remain in the rental unit, based on the tenant's ability to pay all of the rent that is due, or to otherwise fully comply with the lease.

Rent Control Ordinances—Laws in some communities that limit or prohibit rent increases, or that limit the circumstances in which a tenant can be evicted.

Rent Withholding—The tenant's remedy of not paying some or all of the rent if the landlord does not fix defects that make the rental unit uninhabitable within a reasonable time after the landlord receives notice of the defects from the tenant.

Rental Agreement—An oral or written agreement between a tenant and a landlord, made before the tenant moves in, which establishes the terms of the tenancy, such as the amount of the rent and when it is due.

Rental Application—A form that a landlord may ask a tenant to fill out prior to renting that requests information about the tenant, such as the tenant's address, telephone number, employment history, credit references, etc.

Rental Period—The length of time between rental payments; for example, a week or a month.

Rental Unit—An apartment, house, duplex, or condominium that a landlord rents to a tenant to live in.

Renter's Insurance—Insurance protecting the tenant against property losses, such as losses from theft or fire. This insurance usually also protects the tenant against liability for claims or lawsuits filed by the landlord or by others alleging that the tenant negligently injured another person or property.

Repair and Deduct Remedy—The tenant's remedy of deducting from future rent the amount necessary to repair defects covered by the implied warranty of habitability. The amount deducted cannot be more than one month's rent.

Rescission—The cancellation of a contract which returns the parties to the positions they were in before the contract was made.

Residential Hotel—A building containing six or more guest rooms or efficiency units which are rented for occupation or for sleeping purposes by guests, and which also are the primary residence of these guests.

Retaliation—An act by a landlord, such as raising a tenant's rent, seeking to evict a tenant, or otherwise punishing a tenant because the tenant has used the repair and deduct remedy or the rent withholding remedy, or has asserted other tenant rights.

Security Deposit—A deposit or a fee that the landlord requires the tenant to pay at the beginning of the tenancy to protect the landlord, for example, if the tenant moves out owing rent, or leaves the rental unit damaged or less clean than when the tenant moved in.

Service—Legal requirements and procedures that seek to assure that the person to whom a legal notice is directed actually receives it.

Sublease—A separate rental agreement between the original tenant and a new tenant to whom the original tenant rents all or part of the rental unit. The new tenant is called a subtenant. The agreement between the original tenant and the landlord remains in force, and the original tenant continues to be responsible for paying the rent to the landlord and for other tenant's obligations.

Subpoena—An order from the court that requires the recipient to appear as a witness or provide evidence in a court proceeding.

Tenancy—The tenant's exclusive right, created by a rental agreement between the landlord and the tenant, to use and possess the landlord's rental unit.

Tenant—A person who rents or leases a rental unit from a landlord. The tenant obtains the right to the exclusive use and possession of the rental unit during the lease or rental period.

Tenant Screening Service—A business that collects and sells information on tenants, such as whether they pay their rent on time and whether they have been defendants in unlawful detainer lawsuits.

Uninhabitable—A rental unit which has such serious problems or defects that the tenant's health or safety is affected is "uninhabitable." A rental unit may be uninhabitable if it is not fit for human beings to live in, or if it fails to substantially comply with building and safety code standards that materially affect tenants' health and safety.

Unlawful Detainer—In real estate law, the act of a tenant unlawfully retaining possession of the leased premises after the expiration of the lease.

Unlawful Detainer Lawsuit—A lawsuit that a landlord must file and win before he or she can evict a tenant, also called an "eviction" lawsuit.

U.S. Department of Housing and Urban Development—The federal agency that enforces the federal fair housing law, which prohibits discrimination based on sex, race, religion, national or ethnic origin, familial status, or mental handicap.

Waive—To sign a written document—a "waiver"—giving up a right, claim, privilege, etc. In order for a waiver to be effective, the person giving the waiver must do so knowingly, and must know the right, claim, privilege, etc., that he or she is giving up.

Warranty of Habitability—A warranty by a landlord that leased premises are without defects which would render the premises unusable.

Writ of Possession—A document issued by the court after the landlord wins an unlawful detainer lawsuit. The writ of possession is served on the tenant by the sheriff. The writ informs the tenant that the tenant must leave the rental unit within a certain number of days, or the sheriff will forcibly remove the tenant.

Zoning—The government regulation of land use.

BIBLIOGRAPHY AND ADDITIONAL RESOURCES

Black's Law Dictionary, Fifth Edition. St. Paul, MN: West Publishing Company, 1979.

Cornell University Legal Information Institute (Date Visited: October 2006) <http://www.law.cornell.edu>.

Insurance Information Institute. (Date Visited: October 2006) <http://www.iii.org/>.

The Occupational Safety and Health Administration (OSHA) (Date Visited: October 2006) <http://www.osha.gov>.

The United States Environmental Protection Agency (Date Visited: October 2006) <http://www/epa.gov/>.

U.S. Department of Housing and Urban Development (HUD) (Date Visited: October 2006) <http://www.hud.gov>.

The U.S. Department of Housing and Urban Development Office of Fair Housing and Equal Opportunity (Date Visited: October 2006) <http://www.fairhousing.org>.

The U.S. Department of Housing and Urban Development Office of Lead Hazard Control (Date Visited: October 2006) <http://www.hud.gov/lea/leahome.html>.